The Poetry Guide

About the authors

Trevor says...

I started writing poems when I was at school and, thankfully, they have improved since then. After teaching English in the UK and abroad for many years, I managed to juggle a job in educational software with being a writer-in-schools. I became especially interested in how using computers could be used creatively and

that led to lots of articles and some books, included one whose title I was particularly pleased with: *The Mouse and the Muse*. That's the title of my website so if you want to know more about me and my publications, that's where to look: mouseandmuse.co.uk

I also spent some happy years working for Creative Partnerships in primary and secondary schools. It reinforced my belief that you could be creative, have fun and improve children's literacy skills all at the same time.

While working in schools and putting on performances, I was lucky to meet Bernard and we became friends and collaborators. We performed as 'Double Talk' and wrote a poetry collection of that name. Now we're pooling our experiences in this guide for teachers and librarians.

Bernard says...

I've been writing poems and songs since my early teens. It's still what I love to do. I had many enjoyable years as a librarian and began visiting schools and writing poetry for children during that period. I left the profession about 30 years ago to become a full-time poet. Alongside my solo collections I've had poems published in

anthologies in the UK and abroad and some have been broadcast on the radio. As well as visiting hundreds of schools I've performed (often with Trevor as 'Double Talk') at literary festivals, in libraries, prisons, colleges and even in supermarkets!

I'm grateful to a teacher who saw me playing guitar in a show and suggested that the next time she booked me to do some poetry I should bring my guitar. 'The children will love it,' she said. I did as she suggested – she was right. Since then I always include music in my performances and workshops.

If you want to know more about me and my poetry this is my website: bernardyoung.co.uk

The Poetry Guide

A 'How to' Guide for Teachers and Librarians

**TREVOR MILLUM AND
BERNARD YOUNG**

Illustrated by Twink

troika

*For all those teachers and librarians who
continue to make poetry part of children's lives*

Published by TROIKA

First published 2020

Troika Books Ltd,
Well House, Green Lane, Ardleigh CO7 7PD, UK

www.troikabooks.com

A CIP catalogue record for this book is available
from the British Library

ISBN 978-1-912745-09-8

1 3 5 7 9 10 8 6 4 2

Printed in Poland by Totem

Contents

Dear Teacher

We don't know if you're already a poetry enthusiast or someone quite unused to dealing with children and poems. Perhaps you're covering a class for someone and you've been asked to do poetry. Perhaps you're delighted. Perhaps you're terrified… Whatever your feelings are, we hope this book will help.

How will it help?

It will help by not just telling you that 'Poetry is Fun / enjoyable / engaging…' (although it can be all those things) but by providing practical answers to your questions and practical activities for your children to carry out. It will provide real life examples of things actual teachers have done and are doing and which will be achievable in your school unless it is unlike any school which we have taught in or visited – and that's a lot of different schools!

Although our experiences are mainly in England, between us our careers have taken us further afield and we can be pretty sure that what we have to say about children and poetry is appropriate throughout the world where English is the language (or one of the languages) of learning – or indeed beyond. (Trevor's poem, 'Sad I Ams', for example has been taught in Malaysia and translated into Bahasa Malaysia; another has been used in a Swedish text book and Bernard's poems have been published in Germany, Russia and China).

The curriculum requirements of countries, states and provinces differ, as do those of individual schools. Some give quite precise direction as to what should be taught. At one point the English National Curriculum Literacy Hour prescribed, among many other things, a knowledge of clerihews and calligrams. (At the time of writing, 'fronted adverbials' have come to the fore – but not, we believe, within poetry lessons.)

Most, if not all, of what a school is required to teach can be covered quite comfortably within a wide-ranging literacy education. Our hope is that you will want to go far beyond official requirements, particularly in the breadth of poetry children encounter (and the way they encounter it) and in the opportunities they have to write their own.

Poetry is not just an add-on or some kind of special treat. The more that poetry writing and reading become part of children's everyday experience, the better will be their reading and writing, speaking and listening, in other areas of the curriculum.

Do also read the following section addressed to Librarians as it has some useful information about Poetry Days, Festivals and Competitions.

Dear Librarian

Maybe you're a Librarian who reads poetry, maybe you specialise in library work with children, perhaps you write poetry? (Bernard was a librarian who did all of the above but left the profession nearly thirty years ago to become a full-time poet). Possibly, because on this book's cover it says 'A 'How to' Guide for Teachers and Librarians' you thought you'd better check it out in case it contains anything that will assist your work.

We believe it will. You'll find lots of advice about writing poetry (there are plenty of examples of poems that can be used as starting points to get children writing as well as other writing exercises) and also lots of information about reading it, presenting it on the page and online, promoting and performing it.

We're also including some suggestions in this chapter of poetry-related activities and promotions that you could be offering in libraries. Bernard ran the ideas past a previous colleague of his (special thanks here to Kimberley Harston, Librarian at Beverley Library, East Riding of Yorkshire) who says librarians 'should' be doing these things.

Poetry Books

Make sure you stock a full and varied collection. There are many substantial anthologies which offer great value for money (we've listed some of them in the appendices) and every year new collections by individual poets are published. It's worth noting that many poetry books are often slim volumes – their narrow spines mean that they're not seen as well as story books on traditional library shelves and will need to be displayed if they're to attract some attention.

Rhyme Time

Many libraries offer weekly Rhyme Time sessions for the very young that last 20 -30 minutes. BookTrust has this to say:

'Babies and children who discover the pleasure of hearing stories and rhymes have a flying start when it comes to learning to read by themselves. Rhyme Time sessions are organised locally and involve a mix of songs, rhymes, rhythm and movement, while providing the opportunity to share games, books and toys. They are also a friendly, inclusive space for parents and carers to meet up, mingle and make new friends.'

National Poetry Day

This annual event usually falls on the first Thursday in October. A library is the perfect venue to host an event to support it. It's the chance to link up with local schools and have classes visit throughout the day. As poets we love to perform and lead workshops in a room that's full of books. If you can afford to book a professional poet to give readings and/or lead workshops (there might be someone local who wouldn't have any travelling expenses) that's well worth doing. (We have included a chapter on how to get the best out of a visiting poet). You could also book them to give an evening family performance.

You could also host similar events to help celebrate and promote World Book Day which is held on the first Thursday in March each year (though schools are often busy with pupils and staff getting dressed up as their favourite book characters and having visits from authors and poets) and World Poetry Day which is celebrated on March 21st.

Literature Festivals

There are numerous literary festivals that take place every year. Some have library involvement (York Literary Festival has libraries as a partner) and some are entirely organised by the library service. The East Riding Festival of Words in 2018 was devised and run by library staff. They have a small working group whose members each take on a different area of responsibility. However, even if you don't have the funds or the staff to help organise or run a festival you can have events in your libraries and help publicise it.

Poetry Competitions

When Bernard got in touch with Kimberley at Beverley Library she wrote:

'We have reinstated the annual Poetry competition which includes a section for children, obviously a bigger ask but certainly worth mentioning as this can be used to engage local schools.'

Having judged the above competition for several years when he lived in the area, Bernard wholly recommends running one if you can. It attracted entries from children from many schools in the locality and the evening ceremony for prize winners (held in the library) was always a well-attended and heart-warming occasion. The winning poets read out their poems and received prizes. There was a 1st, 2nd and 3rd prize plus a list of highly-commended poems – so quite a number of children won something and received some praise for their writing. You might be able to get a local bookshop or business to provide the prizes.

1 How to...
Encourage Children to Read Poems

I suppose by 'read' we mean 'encounter' as there are many ways to engage with poems (as with all writing). If I listen to a talking book version of *Great Expectations*, can I claim to have 'read' it? (I think I can.) So we can encourage encountering poems through a range of ways.

The most straightforward way for children to encounter poems is by listening. Read them a favourite of yours and do take the trouble to practise beforehand. A well-read poem doesn't just happen, it needs thinking about. See below!

If you're a teacher, this can become a regular thing. It doesn't take much time and children will wonder what you have in store for them today… If you're a librarian, you may only see a group of children briefly but they will appreciate you taking the trouble to share with them. This links to you making the effort to read poetry in your own time. In this way you will come across poems you like and poems you think children of various ages will like.

Children like things to be personal, as you know. Introduce your poem choice with a personal touch. For example, 'I found this poem at the weekend and I really like it…'; 'I wonder if you'll like this one, I found it in an old book of my granddad's'; 'A friend recommended this poem to me. I'm not sure about it. See what you think…'

Visiting poets almost always attract questions about the origin of poems and their responses can be fascinating (and sometimes infuriating) but it shows how the connection between poem and poet helps children to engage.

Sometimes we will take a bit of time to explain how a poem came to be written. 'Exploding Heads' came about because Trevor was a teacher once and got bored standing at the back of assembly, letting his imagination play…

What kind of poems?

All sorts, is the answer. Variation is the key. Sometimes a good long narrative poem such as 'The Highwayman' will be just right, other times a couple of limericks. Nonsense poems by Spike Milligan or Edward Lear are always popular but do try to extend their experience with the odd poem which is outside their usual range, too. There are lots of suggestions at the end of this book, including, of course, some of ours.

Other ways of listening include recordings and videos. These take a bit of research; there are, you will discover, some disappointing readings even by well-known poets and don't bother with those with a robot voice unless you want to point out just how important are the pauses, intonation and all the other qualities of the human voice. On the other hand, sometimes you will come across a YouTube recording by pupils which is just what you're looking for. Again, some suggestions will be found at the end of this book.

Reading poems

Reading a poem is a very different experience to hearing it and every teacher will know that there is a wide range of reading ability in each group. Having a range of poetry collections available is the key here. Children who are not fluent readers will often happily tackle a book of poems, partly because they are usually short, often include illustrations and are quite often funny too. Librarians will know which collections are appropriate for different age and ability ranges and can guide both teachers and children.

In a classroom and in a library, it is possible to inject an extra bit of interest by adding post-it style notes to book shelves – though use something more substantial as actual post-its will curl up and fall like autumn leaves. In bookshops such as Waterstones, staff often add their personal notes about books which always attract curious browsers.

Displaying poems

Poems can be small, shy things. We're not thinking 'Paradise Lost' here or 'Idylls of the King' but texts that very often fit on one side of paper. As a result they need protecting, or rather, they need help to make themselves known. Think about printing poems out in a large font and displaying them around the room. Put them in places where children wouldn't necessarily expect them. We know a teacher who once put a poem in a pupil's lunch box for her to find, the girl in question having shown an interest in a particular poet.

Create a Poetry Wall. This can be a way to have a regularly changing display of poems. Unless you are very organised, changing poems every week will be a counsel of perfection: once a month might work better. A poetry monitor can make things easier, too, if only to remind you that 'The Listeners' has been up for over three weeks… Of course, it should display children's poetry too, but more of that in another section.

2 How to...
Get Them Started Writing a Poem

Facing that blank sheet of paper – so white, so empty – can be a daunting moment, however experienced a writer you are, so even more daunting for children who are beginning to emerge as writers. However, there are lots of ways to kick-start a poem.

One option is to book a poet. Seeing and hearing a professional poet perform/read their own work and then lead some workshops is an excellent way to begin. Of course, you won't be able to afford to do that every day, but the visit will create a momentum and enthusiasm that you'll be able to build on and you can pick up lots of tips and ideas that you'll be able to use in the future. But in this chapter let's concentrate on a bit of D.I.Y.

Where to start

Before they do any writing, introduce the children to a variety of poetry, let them hear and read poems for themselves and examine, with you, how a poem has been put together because patterns or structures are a great help in writing. They help you to know where you're going and support you when you get there. Trevor has a poem called 'Ten Little Schoolchildren' which is a good one to try:

> *Ten little schoolchildren*
> *Standing in a line.*
> *One opened her mouth too far*
> *And then there were nine.*

It doesn't have to be schoolchildren and it doesn't have to be ten – try beginning with five or six and follow that pattern until you end up with none/zero/nil/zilch.

There's certainly no need to be shy about using other people's poems as an inspiration for your own. After reading a poem by Roger McGough about when to cut your fingernails (it ends on a Sunday with your nails growing as long as your hair!) Bernard wrote two poems – 'When To Cut Your Hair' and 'When To Tease Your Sister':

15

Tease her on Monday
She'll go mad
Tease her on Tuesday
She'll be sad
(See Appendix *for the full poem*)

That model could be used to write a poem about when to go to school, when to play football, when to go dancing etc. It's nice and simple, works well with or without rhyme and is a suitable poem for younger children to attempt.

Some other structures you're likely to be familiar with are:

Haiku - A haiku usually has 17 syllables and 3 lines arranged in a 5, 7, 5 syllable pattern.

Cinquain - A cinquain has 22 syllables and 5 lines arranged in a 2, 4, 6, 8, 2 pattern

Acrostic – A poem in which the first (or the last) letters of each line spell a word or sentence.

If you dip into some of the numerous anthologies available, you're likely to discover many well-crafted poems which make use of patterns or structures.

Class/Group Poems

A joint effort is another way to ease children into writing their own poems. If writing is a collaborative effort, it takes the pressure off the less confident children. When you first begin brainstorming and gathering ideas, writing them up on a flip-chart or whiteboard, the same few hands will go up. However, as confidence grows, more and more children will be offering up their ideas and the room will come alive with enthusiasm and creativity.

Group writing works very well if you're trying to write a poem on a particular topic. We've recently created class poems on Freedom, Road Safety, Vikings, Materials (linen, glass, plastic), Superheroes, and Famous Historical Figures.

First, discuss the subject, gather some facts, write them up for everyone to see. One idea leads to another, one word triggers another; one child's suggestion might give the poem its first line, another child might say something that provides a chorus. Do encourage any adults in the room to join in too. This is a group effort.

Once, when attempting to compose a class Road Safety poem, a boy put his hand up and quoted the Green Cross Code – *Stop! Look! Listen! Think!* Repeated twice that became the refrain:

> *Stop! Look! Listen! Think!*
> *Stop! Look! Listen! Think!*

It also gave us the idea to write four verses (one about stopping, the next about looking etc.) with the refrain appearing after each verse. Suddenly we'd got a structure and a pattern to follow.

You can apply the same method to any topic.

> *Marie Curie*
> *Marie Curie*
> *We want to tell you all about Marie Curie*

We've found that it's possible (and great fun) to create a group poem in just under 30 minutes. If you've got 45 minutes, that's even better and in 60 minutes you can have written, rehearsed and performed a poem involving a whole class (even two classes). Result!

When children first begin writing their own poems it can be beneficial to keep it short and simple. To finish a poem by the end of a lesson/workshop is very encouraging. It's early days – you want them to have some fun, to experience the pleasure of playing with words, to discover a love of language, to learn how to explore its possibilities and make it work for them.

A Few Tips

The title doesn't have to be the first thing they write. Some children feel they can't make a start unless they've got one. The best titles often come after the poem is finished. Sometimes a line or a few words from the poem become the title. (If they're desperate tell them to use a 'working title').

They can guess how to spell a word rather than interrupt the flow by checking a dictionary or asking a teacher. Spellings can be corrected later.

And so can punctuation!

In one classroom Bernard visited he heard children being told that every line must start with a capital letter and that a comma must be placed at the end of each line. Oh dear. It's true that some poets do set their poems out like that. Some follow the normal prose rules regarding punctuation while others use very little. Some of our performance poems use no punctuation:

> *My very famous feet*
> *Are walking down the street*
> *Goal-scorers*
> *Crowd-pleasers*
> *My very famous feet*

(from 'Very Famous Feet' by Bernard Young in *What Are You Like?*)

Don't put barriers in their way before they've even written a word. The finer details can be sorted later. Concentrate on releasing the energy and encouraging the creativity. Let the poetry begin. It's exciting!

3 More Ideas for Writing a Poem

Two poets, Two voices

Bernard often bases a writing workshop
on his poem 'Brilliant':

> *Today Mum called me brilliant*
> *and that's just how I feel*
>
> *I'll run a race*
> *I'm bound to win*
> *I'll take up golf*
> *Get a hole in one*
>
> *Because today Mum called me brilliant*
> *so that's what I must be*
>
> *(See* Appendix *for the full poem.)*

Having performed the poem (listeners usually join in with the word
'brilliant' each time it appears) he shows them the pattern it follows
and suggests that, rather than having mum call them brilliant (even
though, of course, they are) they write a poem called 'Today I'm
Feeling…' and that they work with a partner. The aim is to compose
a poem suitable for two voices. He asks for words to describe how
someone might be feeling on any particular day. 'Happy, lively, lazy,
angry, quiet' are suggested. He selects 'quiet' and asks what might
someone do, how might they behave, if they're in a quiet mood?

> *Stay in bed. Hide in a corner.*
> *Whisper. Read a book. Creep around.*
> *Tiptoe everywhere.*

So the first draft could be:

> *Today I'm feeling quiet*
> *So that's what I will be*
> *I'll hide in a corner*
> *I'll read a book*
> *When I go*
> *I will tiptoe*
> *Because today I'm feeling quiet*

The idea is that the next person is feeling the opposite to quiet so words to illustrate that are required. *'Loud.' 'Shouty.' 'Thunderous.' 'Noisy.' 'Deafening.'*

> *Today I'm feeling noisy*
> *So that's what I will be*
> *I'll bang on doors*
> *I'll thump down the stairs*
> *I'll holler at the top of my voice*
> *I'll make the windows rattle*
> *Because today I'm feeling noisy*

This is a poem of opposites and is very effective when performed. The pairs can help one other with each verse but then split the verses between them when it's performed. You get a whispered 'quiet' verse followed by a very loud (loud enough to make the audience jump) 'noisy' verse. Then there could be a slow yawny 'lazy' verse followed by a manic 'lively' one. Two verses each and a final fifth verse, spoken together, is an option to consider.

The 'Brilliant' model has been used in schools to promote positive behaviour where words such as kind, helpful, considerate, sensible and thoughtful work well.

The Dark Avenger

This is a much anthologised poem of Trevor's and an excellent model to base some writing on. It can be written with a partner and performed as a duo. In Trevor's poem the dog owner presents some rather grand ideas – 'My dog is called The Dark Avenger' – whereas the beast in question gives a more down to earth version of what's going on – 'Hello, I'm Cuddles'.

> There was a pale menacing figure ahead of us
> *Then I saw the white Scottie from next door*
>
> Avenger sprang into battle, eager to defend her master
> *Never could stand terriers*
>
> They fought like tigers
> *We scrapped like dogs*
>
> *(See* Appendix *for the full poem.)*

This model offers an opportunity to have some fun with everyday happenings such as playtime/lunchtime, a football match, a visit to the dentist, travelling to school…

Hasten, let us journey to the Palace of Wisdom
Get in the car or we'll be late for school

We must travel through dangerous terrain
There are a couple of busy roundabouts
and a sharp left turn before we arrive
and some parents park where they shouldn't!

Cinquains

As mentioned in the previous chapter, a cinquain has 22 syllables and 5 lines arranged in a 2, 4, 6, 8, 2 pattern.

Tell the children you'd like them to write about a pet. It can be an imaginary one or one they own. If imagined it can be any creature. They need to jot down plenty of information eg. colour of skin/fur, size, what it eats, any unusual or amusing habits it has, the sounds it makes – does it purr, growl, screech? Is it friendly, scary, timid, daft?

This should result in the children having a lot of words in front of them, perhaps enough for several animal poems, but tell them that they're only going to be able to use 22 syllables. Ooh, a challenge.

You'll need to show them an example of a cinquain. An anthology, published by Macmillan, called *The Works* has a section devoted to them and you will be able to find many examples online. You could, of course, have a go at this yourself and show the children what you've written. Here's a pet one by Bernard. (He used to have a cat called Edith. She was over 18 years old when she died. She was a Devon Rex and didn't have much fur so liked heat. She was really keen on her food and, like most cats, enjoyed some fuss when it suited her).

My cat
is old. All she
wants is food, warmth and a
comfy knee. My cat's a home bird.
Like me.

('Birds of a Feather' by Bernard Young in *What Are You Like?*)

There is the option of giving the pet a two syllable name so that it can be the first or last line (or even the first and last line). If anyone has an elephant at home called Archibald they can call it Archie. If they've got a fish called Wanda that's perfect.

Getting familiar with patterns such as cinquains (and other concise poems, such as haiku and tanka) is invaluable. It helps with economy of language. Every word must count so it's an excellent exercise in editing and honing your writing. It's a good idea to count syllables on fingers when writing and then changes can be made as the poem progresses. Cinquains often don't rhyme but there's nothing to say they can't. They can, of course, be about anything.

Dear Bad Mood

Ask the children to write a poem in the form of a letter (or email). As usual, it's a good idea to share a few examples with them before they begin. Bernard has written several, including a message from a depressed tortoise who won't come out of his shell and a letter to 'The Great Provider' from Montague Mouse saying thank you for providing the cheese but 'would it be possible to place it/by the side of our hole/ and not on the spikes/of the thing that snaps/when we take a bite?'

He's written one to a teacher too:

> ### Absent
>
> *Dear Teacher,*
> *my body's arrived*
> *it sits at a table*
> *a pen in its hand*
> *as if it is able*
> *to think and to act*
> *perhaps write down the answer*
> *to the question you've asked*
>
> *but don't let that fool you.*
>
> *My mind is elsewhere.*
> *My thoughts far away.*
>
> *So apologies, teacher,*
> *I'm not here today.*
>
> ('Absent' by Bernard Young, in *What Are You Like?*)

The letter poems can be to anyone or anything – Dear Diary, Dear Moon, Dear Dinosaur, Dear Mobile Phone ('Since I lost you/I'm missing you so much./Please get in touch.'). They could write to their future selves and offer some good advice. They could write to an emotion or mood:

Dear Bad Mood,
You spoil my day.
I want you to go away.
That is really all I have to say.

Yours sincerely,
Joy.

4 How to help them edit

'My children will happily write poems,' said one Y5 teacher, 'but getting them to edit them is hard work!' Why should we be surprised? Do you enjoy editing and redrafting after you've written something? Probably not. So children need help and encouragement to see that editing is an essential part of writing and particularly, we would say, when writing poems. Poems are by their nature usually short and often very condensed. If you are only using a small number of words, it's even more important to make sure that they really are the ones you want – 'the best words in the best order' (Coleridge).

It's not always easy for children to understand what is meant by editing or redrafting. It could just mean correcting any spelling mistakes and writing out more neatly. Our way of explaining it is to break it down into the following possibilities:

- Deleting words
- Adding words
- Changing words
- Moving words

In all these cases, 'words' could well mean whole lines of a poem.

Deleting

It's not a bad thing to get a lot of ideas down on paper to begin with as long as it's clear that not all of them will make the final poem. It can be hard to remove something you've written, especially if you are a slow writer, but often it has to be done. Some children (and adults) simply write too much. It may be that a word or phrase adds nothing new ('the big enormous cat') or is simply irrelevant to the meaning of the lines. Don't confuse this with *deliberate* repetition, though ('Be afraid. Be very afraid!')

Adding

More rarely, words may need to be added. This might be to make the meaning clearer, more interesting or pleasanter to hear. Sometimes even an extra syllable can make all the difference to a line. Don't overdo the use of so-called 'wow' words; these can make a poem sound as if the writer prefers to read a thesaurus rather than other poems. This opening:

> *My sister has a cat*
> *It likes to sit and purr on her lap*

would be improved by a simple appropriate adjective, such as lovely or ginger, adding detail but also balancing the line.

A word about cliché

Cliched expressions may be obvious to us but emerging writers have not got our experience and long memory! They may not realise that a phrase is long worn out and 'as cold as ice', for instance, is no longer very effective. Try not to squash the enthusiasm of the writer but gently suggest alternatives.

Changing

Altering what you've written is basic to all forms of composition. A first choice of words is not always the best and, on consideration, better alternatives might well be found. Remember, children's individual vocabularies (their idiolect) will be smaller than yours and should be helped *gradually* to expand. If they are supplied with too many new and unfamiliar words at once, the result is indigestion. A thesaurus is a useful tool but its use should follow some thought and perhaps discussion rather than precede it.

Moving

Moving words is easy when one is using a computer. On paper, it is trickier. This is a shame because moving a line to another place in a poem can make all the difference. Also, the opportunity a computer gives to try things out is an enormous benefit… However, most of the time children will be working with pencil and paper so a recommendation we always make is to write on every other line. This leaves a space for words to be added or changed, or for whole lines to be inserted. This is a simple technique too often ignored or forgotten.

> sad?
> The 'hurt ' little boy crying
>   yard
> in the ~~playground~~ .
>   first
> (The) babys ^ birthday
>   single
> without a ^card .

The writer David Almond takes his notebook with him when visiting schools in order to show them how messy his work is – full of crossings out, insertions and arrows. You might like to do the same with something you've written; they don't need to be able to read it – just see enough to get the message that very few things are correct (or at their best) when they are first written down – including this chapter!

See also the section on 'Sharing' in *How to make Technology work for you*.

5 Imagery, similes, metaphors and all that

Depending on where you live, your schools' curricula may define what children 'need to know' about poetry and about literary terms in particular. Some will even say at what age certain terms should be taught. We believe that the 'naming of parts' in poetry (and indeed in other texts) can seriously harm the way in which children view and appreciate poetry.

Children create vivid images for themselves without knowing they've made a metaphor and will read a description with delight without knowing it was an example of personification. At some point in their development it will be appropriate for these things to be made explicit – but let that rest until they are older, if you can.

In the meantime, make sure that they experience and enjoy all the word play and technical tricks that poets get up to. You can mention that 'lonely as a cloud' is a simile if you like but don't labour it. They know that the moon isn't a balloon, you don't need to inform them that it's a metaphor. Similarly, they know the kite isn't actually a magic bird…

Our kite was a magic bird
And the wind took it into the sky,
Above our heads, above the trees,
Flying way up high.

But the wind was a thief
Who wanted our kite,
It tugged and tugged
With all its might.

And the wind was a blade
That could cut anything,
It took our kite
And left us the string.

(From 'Lost Kite' by Brian Moses)

They will also know that Charlie's ears aren't really shells, though the use of 'like' makes the distinction clearer. Sometimes we poets use 'as' or 'like' when creating a comparison and sometimes we don't. It's just what feels best at the time in the context of the sound or the meaning of the poem.

> *Charlie's ears are like delicate shells –*
> *They're smaller than Ella's or Isabelle's*

(from 'Ears' by Hilda Offen)

You can use examples like these to encourage children's appreciation of imagery and inspire them to think up images of their own. More examples can be found at the end of this book.

A poem that has worked well as a way into creating innovative imagery is through 'Sad I Ams':

> *I am*
>> *the ring*
>> *from an empty soda can*
>> *the scrapings*
>> *from an unwashed porridge pan*
>> *the severed arm*
>> *of last year's Action Man*
>
> *I am*
>> *the envelope*
>> *on which the gum is gone*
>> *the sticky tape*
>> *where you can't find the end*
>> *the toothless stapler, the inkless pen*
>> *the dried up liquid paper*
>> *that mars instead of mends*
>> *the stamped addressed reply*
>> *that you forgot to send*
>
> *I am*
>> *a garden*
>> *overgrown with weeds*
>> *a library book*
>> *that no one ever reads*

> *a stray*
> *which no one thinks to feed*
> *the piece of good advice*
> *which no one seems to need.*

(by Trevor Millum from *Too Much Schooling Can Damage Your Health*)

In groups, children come up with their own list of 'sad I ams' and then share them with the others. From these a composite list is made, which must include at least one line from each child. This will comprise a verse. Combine all the verses from the groups and you have a poem. You will need to make clear that we are talking sad, not suicidal. Otherwise, 'I am an aircraft plunging to the earth' will not be an unusual kind of response. If children are stuck, offer some themes they might like to use. For example, sport. 'I am a racket with a broken string' or 'I am the goal without a net'. Clothing, food and animals are also good starting points. You can try 'Glad I Ams' also, of course, though, strangely, we've found them less effective.

Alternatively, picture someone else:

> *She's a fragile ghost*
> *She's a white angel*
> *She's scruffy trainers and tight jeans*
> *She's diet coke and burnt toast*

(from 'Anna' by Roger Stevens in *Poetry Zone*)

A variation on these images created through comparisons is personification. (At least this has a clear meaning: made into or acting like a person.) Children can have fun with these too with or without knowing the terminology. From 'The sun smiled on them' to 'The angry waves beat at the shore', it's obvious what's happening and no one needs to have the workings of the machine exposed.

Try playing a matching game, like this, to create interesting images:

did what?

the

angry	tree
stubborn	rock
lonely	waves
cunning	cloud
snarling	path
showy	sum
laughing	motorbike

The idea is to match an adjective with a noun and then complete the phrase with an action. For example,

'The snarling motorbike ignored the rest of the traffic.'

See if anyone can come up with an unusual connection; why might the path be cunning or the tree showy, for instance? The examples are just to get you started – and, don't do all the work yourself, get the children to come up with items for their own table.

Some poems are laden with similes, metaphors, personification. Others use none but can be equally effective. Think how little there is in 'Cargoes', a poem that conjures up so many pictures in the reader's mind. At its best, imagery comes naturally. It's only afterwards you notice that, for example, a simile has appeared.

6 How to answer 'What does it mean?'

It's natural that children should ask 'What does that mean?' when they encounter something unfamiliar and a bit puzzling. Sometimes the question can be answered quite easily – for example, if it is a matter of vocabulary or a geographical location. On other occasions it might be that with a little rearrangement of the words in the line, the meaning becomes clear. To take an example you probably won't be sharing with your children, but which makes the point:

'For thy sweet love remembered such wealth brings' could be rephrased 'Remembering thy sweet love brings such wealth' or to make it even clearer, 'When I remember thy sweet love, it brings such wealth.' (Shakespeare's 'Sonnet 29')

Also, simple expressions, once common, may need explanation, eg. 'receipted bills' and 'holiday snaps to enlarge'.

> *Receipted bills and invitations*
> *To inspect new stock or to visit relations*
>
> *...News circumstantial, news financial,*
> *Letters with holiday snaps to enlarge in...*

(from *The Night Mail* by W H Auden)

Reading 'The Highwayman', you might be asked what a 'cocked hat' is. An image search will bring up a French cocked-hat, pistol butts and a rapier hilt: clearer explanations than any words:

> *He'd a French cocked-hat on his forehead,*
> *a bunch of lace at his chin,*
> *A coat of the claret velvet,*
> *and breeches of brown doe-skin*
>
> *...His pistol butts a-twinkle,*
> *His rapier hilt a-twinkle, under the jewelled sky.*

(from 'The Highwayman' by Alfred Noyes)

However, sometimes there is something more complex in the poem that does need explanation. Mostly, you will be able to clarify it but sometimes you will be foxed yourself. What to do when that happens?

Don't panic. No one can know everything. Poems, even those in anthologies for younger readers, can contain quirks, references or idiosyncrasies which one doesn't immediately (or sometimes, ever) understand.

Poets write in a compressed form and often expect the reader to do more work than a prose writer might. Sometimes the poet him or herself might not fully know why that phrase came to be written! Take Coleridge's famous *Kubla Khan*, for example, from which these lines are taken.

> *A damsel with a dulcimer*
> *In a vision once I saw*
> *It was an Abyssinian maid,*
> *And on a dulcimer she played,*
> *Singing of Mount Abora*

Plenty has been written about Abyssinian maid and Mount Abora – but does it really make a difference to the enjoyment of the poem to know the possible references? Is some mystery, in fact, a bonus?

Let's assume you're aware of some difficulties in a poem and you've done your best to work things out but without success. You may want to bring this up or wait until someone asks. If no one asks, do you ignore it and move on, reasoning that there's no point in introducing problems if it's not necessary? If you or they do raise the issue, admit that you're a bit stumped. Ask for suggestions and be prepared to settle for 'perhaps…' or 'I wonder if…'

Similarly, if a poem is brought to you with things in it you don't understand, use whatever reference materials are available or ask them to do the same. If that doesn't work, you'll have to settle for 'perhaps…' once again.

All this has pros and cons. On the one hand, children do want an answer. They find it difficult to accept that you don't know or that it's unknowable. However, the advantage is that you can share the fact that (a) you don't know everything, no one does, and (b) that some things might only be understood by the poet or by some kind of literary expert. This is good for them.

At this stage of their school life, children should be able to enjoy poems without worrying over much about every bit of meaning. There is enough of that when they reach GCSEs or their equivalent.

> 'Kubla Khan is as near enchantment, I suppose, as we are like to come in this dull world.'
>
> J L Lowes 1927

Poems can work simply through their overall effect, especially if read aloud, and can be enjoyed without our always straining after meaning. Reading Kubla Khan or the witches' chant from Macbeth to a group should bear this out.

And, of course, there are plenty of Nonsense Poems available, where no one has to be concerned at all about what things mean because it's all daft. That doesn't mean that a Nonsense Poem is easy to write – but that's another story...

7 How to do Poetry with pre-readers / writers

Can you do poetry with children who are not yet able to write or to read? Of course you can. You can read them all sorts of great poems. But how can you get them not just to be passive listeners but active participants?

Joining In

Children love joining in. They will happily fill in the gaps in well-known chants and rhymes. Cumulative poems are also good for this, such as 'This is the house that Jack built' which begins:

> *This is the house that Jack built.*
> *This is the malt that lay in the house that Jack built.*
> *This is the rat that ate the malt*
> *That lay in the house that Jack built.*
> *This is the cat*
> *That killed the rat that ate the malt*
> *That lay in the house that Jack built.*
> (and so on…)

Trevor has a similar poem 'One Worm Working' which also brings in alliteration and number and can be found in the Appendix along with the poem below.

From repeating lines, the next step is for them to suggest words and phrases themselves. Trevor's 'Valerie Malory and Sue Hu Nu' begins

> *Valerie Malory and Sue Hu Nu*
> *Went to school with a kangaroo*
> *Half way there and half way back*
> *They met a duck with half a quack.*

'Went to school with a …' provides an opening for many alternatives and an opportunity to play with rhyme and rhythm if you wish. There are lots of animals ending with the 'oo' sound. (Cockatoo, shrew, ewe, gnu, cow that went moo…) But the item doesn't have to be an animal of course. If children suggest a single syllable word, try it out. Do they hear something not quite right? Would 'old brown shoe' sound better than 'shoe' on its own? Of course, Sue's name can be changed too in order to give more options.

Creating their own: The Magic Box

A technique we have often used is based around the idea of a magic box, inspired by a poem by Kit Wright. Into this box you can put anything, from a teddy bear to a sunset. The children suggest things and you write them on the board or flip chart. If they are pre-readers, this is just for your benefit. All suggestions are accepted – then you start to organise them. You're looking for a couple of words that rhyme. It's not as hard as you might think. If 'teddy bear' has, for example, been put forward, anything 'to share' will do nicely. You might come up with a verse such as this:

A football shirt
And a teddy bear
A nice spring day
And a cake to share.

Your children may be able to hear the rhythm and suggest how to make the lines sound right. If not, you can add the odd syllable to make it all work. The poem (or chant) goes like this:

In the Box, in the Magic Box
In the Box, in the Magic Box
There's a football shirt
And a teddy bear
A nice spring day
And a cake to share.
In the Box, in the Magic Box
In the Box, in the Magic Box

And so on to the next verse. If they can remember the lines or read some of them, they can join throughout. Otherwise they can simply do the chorus. It's fun to finish with several repeats of 'In the Box, in the Magic Box' getting quieter and quieter and then a very loud one to end with.

The format of 'Ten Little Schoolchildren' (see 'How to Get Them Started Writing a Poem') can be adapted ad infinitum and can be used as a joining in poem or one where they start to create their own verses.

> *Ten little schoolchildren*
> *Standing in a line.*
> *One opened her mouth too far*
> *And then there were nine.*
>
> *Nine little schoolchildren*
> *Trying not to be late.*
> *One missed the school bus*
> *And then there were eight.*

(See Appendix for the full poem)

It's the second and third lines which change (apart from the numbers in lines one and four) and the second line needs to rhyme with the final number. Luckily there are many rhymes for numbers one to nine (except for seven – I've used eleven, heaven and Devon and you may find others; a 'near rhyme' will do!)

Creating their own: I Like What I Like

When working with the Early Years age group Bernard performs a simple list poem called 'I Like What I Like'

> *I like coffee*
> *I like tea*
> *I like the sand*
> *I like the sea*
> *I like to sink*
> *into my old settee*
> *I like what I like*
> *I do*
>
> *I like honey*
> *on my bread*
> *I like sleeping*
> *in my bed*
> *I like dreaming*
> *in my head*

I like what I like
I do

(*See* Appendix *for the full poem*)

Ask the children to think of things that they like and make a list of their suggestions. Tell them it can be anything - food perhaps, maybe something to do with school or home, games they like to play, animals/pets. If the first child to answer says 'dogs' you may well find you get nothing but animals so you will need to steer them onto other topics if you want some variety. You could group the answers though and have an animal verse, a food verse, a school verse etc.

I like dogs
I like cats
I like snakes
I like bats
I like elephants
I like rats

I like what I like
I do

You could change the 'I' to 'We' as it's a group poem and you don't have to rhyme:

We like playing
We like friends
We like singing
We like cakes
We like our teacher
and we like our school

We like what we like
We do

Bernard adds some guitar to this one. It sounds great (with or without guitar) when performed and it's even better when a few (not too many) actions are included.

Finally

So whenever you come across a poem with a clear pattern, think how you might use it for this kind of work which, in our experience, children really enjoy: both creating and performing.

8 How to use a variety of stimuli to encourage writing

The best stimulus for writing is the visit of a writer – but we would say that, wouldn't we! However true that might be, it's not going to happen often, so it's worth thinking about other forms of stimulus you might employ.

Sound

Sound effects

Sound is a very powerful stimulus because it allows children's imaginations a fuller reign than when accompanied by pictures. Unlike a still image there is no such thing as a still sound – it must have duration. Therefore, if the sound clip is long enough, children can be jotting down ideas /thoughts while listening and, anyway, it can be repeated.

There are a number of resource banks available, including the comprehensive BBC Sound Archive: bbcsfx.acropolis.org.uk/ and Freesound: freesound.org In both of these, you can search for the kind of sound you want, from machines operating to wind whistling through trees to footsteps in the snow…

Soundscapes are collections of sounds usually with a theme. Using a variety of instruments, toys, kitchen implements and workshop kit, you can create your own. Even better, a group of children can do so with the simplest of recording equipment. Great fun if you have the time. If not, here are two soundscapes – downloadable from mouseandmuse.co.uk/writingrecordings

Recorded music

The world is your oyster here. Again, look for music with which the children are not likely to be familiar and preferably without lyrics so that they can more easily imagine themselves into the atmosphere created. There are some examples at the end of this chapter. You will find much more once you start exploring.

Film music can be useful in this context. A search for film music or movie soundtracks will open up an Aladdin's Cave. With tags such as 'Emotional and Relaxing Drama & Epic Film Music', how can you go wrong? The only drawback is the time you will spend deciding which to use.

You have your sound or music clips but children will still need direction.

You might offer some of these prompts. Imagine yourself surrounded by the music. What do you feel? What would the sound feel like if you could touch it? What shape and colour is the sound? What does it remind you of? If the sound was a person, what kind of person would they be? (Or, if the sound was a place, where would it be?) If this was the background to a film, what might be happening? And so on.

These kinds of prompts can be spoken, leaving a relatively short time for a quick written response. This prevents children lingering too long over one question. Afterwards, the questions can be displayed. The notes they write at this point will not (usually) comprise a poem but will provide the raw material for one. You might like to refer to the chapter on editing at this point. (See also: 'How to make use of music'.)

Vision

Still images

There are a whole host of images you can track down on the internet. Search with a phrase such as 'images for creative writing'. onceuponapicture.co.uk and literacyshed.com/the-images-shed. are definitely worth a look. As long as you don't reproduce them for use outside your library or classroom, such images will be copyright free.

When you want to provide a stimulus for poetry writing, try to choose images which are not too specific; in other words, pictures which will stimulate children's imaginations rather than providing a ready-made outcome.

You might use one image for everyone or print out postcard sized images to be distributed to individuals or pairs. We have been collecting interesting postcards for years and now have a wide and very useful collection.

Again, children will need some guidance. Many images will very readily lend themselves to story-writing ('What happens next?' and 'How did they get to be there?' are great starters) but less obviously to poetry writing. (See text box below)

As with the music stimulus, you could provide prompts. For example, 'Imagine you are in the picture. What can you hear and smell? Touch something; what is it? How does it feel? What can you see in the distance? Do you like being there or not – how do you feel? What are you hoping for? What are you afraid of?' Don't forget that children may have suggestions for prompts, too.

Photographs

Real photos, especially old ones, can be powerful imagination triggers. These will often be of people and so lend themselves naturally to imagined biographies. Encourage children to write short precise phrases unless you want the writing to turn into prose stories. This will need some practice and the experience of some examples.

Moving images

The same advice applies to moving images as to stills, only more so. A video will almost always have some kind of narrative running through it and you don't want children to just retell the story. A video of landscapes (or town or seascape) can work well, though.

> Of course, a poem can tell a story, but most children will find it hard to sustain a narrative in a poem. By all means let them try. Using images from a book, photographed and put into PowerPoint, Trevor retold the story of Ulysses and the Cyclops to a class of 8-9 year olds. He modelled the writing of simple four-line ballad verses and then divided the story up into sections, which were distributed to the children. They worked in groups, each group tasked to produce one or two verses. The verses were assembled and the result was the complete story in ballad form. They were very pleased with themselves!

All the senses

Visits

Even the simplest out of school experience can lead to great writing. Trevor worked in an inner-city school which was near a small park. They had listened to poems about autumn, including classics like Keats 'To Autumn' just to establish a mood. One autumn morning, the teacher took her class for a walk in the park, simply asking them to observe. They could jot down notes but it wasn't mandatory. On return, they jotted down their recollections and turned them into poems. The results were quite amazing, so different from the cliched verses of previous attempts. Observation, observation, observation…

Objects

Small, simple objects can also be used to stimulate thought and imagination. A chess piece, a mirror, a china ornament, a toy, a bracelet… Collect interesting articles over time and they will come in handy both for poetry writing and story writing. Pose some questions. What is your object, where did it come from, what can it do, what does it make you think of…and so on.

A silver bracelet
Shiny starry
On my arm it jingles
And tingles
And then the little people come
Landing like butterflies
On my wrist

Writer Ed Boxall (author of *Me and My Alien Friend*) has his own 'Bureau of Creative Investigation', which, he says, 'Is literally a small Victorian Bureau full of letters, boxes, pictures and objects - all with linking poetry and drawing activities. The pictures in the suitcase are linked to an activity based on my poem "The Twilight Dragon" where children turn an atmospheric landscape painting into a mythical creature and write a poem describing the creature.'

Looking into Ed Boxall's box

Namaste Music: Flute Meditation youtube.com/watch?v=9BD1y0TOk3o
Call of the Winds: youtube.com/watch?v=384wt6tznwE
Gamelan from Java: youtube.com/watch?v=mwLv6SwjWVs
The Beatles - Flying: youtu.be/Z1ONJQLdZrk
Nick Cave & Warren Ellis - The Proposition: youtu.be/8-7WbXwhOoM
London Philharmonic Orchestra - Exodus: youtu.be/XjA7pRD6P_I

9 How to combine poetry and music

Poetry and music are very good friends – Nikki Giovanni

Bernard always takes a guitar along when he visits schools. It adds another element to his performance and assists in engaging a young audience. Children, so he's been told, think it's 'cool' to have someone standing in front of them playing a guitar. He often makes use of it in workshops too.

However, Bernard (by his own admission) is no singer, and although children sometimes refer to his guitar poems as songs, he considers them to be poems with some guitar accompaniment. He speaks rather than sings the words.

But does there need to be a dividing line? Does it matter whether we call something a lyric or a poem when we're trying to introduce children to the pleasure to be found in the creative use of language? We would say not.

Obviously there are many lyrics which only do the job they're designed for, i.e. they sound great and work well with music but can appear weak (and don't always make sense) when they stand alone. But there have been many popular songwriters who do write lyrics that many consider to be poetry – Bob Dylan is an obvious example, particularly when you consider the fact that he was awarded the Nobel Prize for Literature in 2016.

Poetry began as an oral art form. Poems, like songs, were heard rather than read. Both forms have beats and rhythms and, often as not, they make use of rhyme. There are structural similarities too - verses and refrains are a common element.

> *When we set off*
> *Six hours ago*
> *We never imagined*
> *We'd feel this low*
>
> *Traffic jam*
> *Traffic jam*
> *We're all stuck in a traffic jam*

Mum is grumbling
Dad is growling
My brother's moaning
And I feel like howling

Traffic jam
Traffic jam
We're all stuck in a traffic jam

(from 'Traffic Jam' by Bernard Young in *What Are You Like?*)

'Traffic Jam' was written as a performance poem, has been published in several books and performed hundreds of times without music. Many years after its publication Bernard added the guitar accompaniment. (It uses 5 chords – E minor, A minor, G, D, A).

If you do play an instrument, and many teachers do (in classrooms we've seen plenty of guitars that belong to teachers and many schools provide guitar and/or ukulele lessons for pupils) it's worth considering whether you can make use of that skill in poetry related lessons. Guitars and ukuleles are ideal instruments for this purpose. They're easier to recite to than a violin or a saxophone and they're much easier to carry around than a piano!

Workshops

In workshops the guitar proves itself to be a useful tool (particularly when composing a class poem). It helps to stimulate ideas and speeds up the writing process. Quite what you decide to play depends on how proficient you are. You might be able to come up with a catchy riff to start things off but keeping it simple and strumming just two or three chords (many wonderful songs have been written using only a few chords) immediately provides a pattern or structure. (We've talked about the importance of structures and patterns elsewhere. You soon find out if a line is too awkward or too long when you try reciting it to the musical accompaniment and it effortlessly illustrates the need to edit and hone the work to fit what's being played.

Here's an example of how a guitar-based workshop with a whole class might go using a chord sequence that will be easy for a beginner:

Strum a C chord. Ask the children to listen to the rhythm and see if they're inspired to come up with some words. Someone offers

I was walking down the road on my way to school

OK. We can start with that, but listen to what's being played. The music ends before the words finish. However, 'I was walking down the road' is an exact fit. If the chord is strummed for twice as long we can say

I was walking down the road
I was on my way to school

Looks as though four lines will be needed to finish the verse and that 7 syllable lines appear to work. We're getting bored with that C chord though. Change to F for the third line. Someone suggests

My friend was up ahead

That sounds fine. Only 6 syllables but it works and, as the chord changes, introduces another character into the scenario. The natural thing is to go back to the C chord for the fourth line. A rhyme with school would sound good. Unsurprisingly 'Cool' is suggested. There might be a better rhyme out there but this is just the first draft so we accept cool and get 'He was trying to look cool'.

We test what we've got:

C
I was walking down the road
C
I was on my way to school
F
My friend was up ahead
C
He was trying to look cool

An everyday scene. Now we want to make it more interesting. Strum the following chord progression - G, F, C, G - ask for some ideas about what happens next. Perhaps a spaceship will appear or a strange creature:

G
Then from out of nowhere
F
I heard a massive roar
C
I looked up at the sky
G
And this is what I saw...

Because Bernard is a guitarist and has plenty of experience in leading guitar-based poetry workshops we've concentrated on that instrument. If you play something else it would be worth experimenting and seeing what results you get.

The use of percussion is another option. You could ask a few children (you don't want to drown out the voices) to clap their hands or tap on their desks:

(Clap-clap-clap-clap)

Start beating that drum
Clap-clap-clap-clap
Start singing that song

Finally

If you don't play an instrument, why not use recorded instrumental music to generate some ideas? It provides a structure for the writing and triggers an emotional response.

See 'Using a variety of stimuli for writing'.

10 How to use audio / video as an aid

As with much of technology, there are two different but complementary ways of viewing audio and video as a resource. One is passive in essence; i.e. children watch or listen. The other is active in that they are engaged in the process, whether recording themselves or being recorded. Both have their part to play in the enjoyment of poetry.

Watching or Listening

As we have seen ('How to Encourage Children to Read Poems') it is possible to find both audio and video recordings of poems online. They vary in quality. Some are not read very well and some are even voiced using 'robot speech' – not the best way to encounter poetry! Therefore, it's important to research recordings carefully.

For older children, a task might be for them to research recordings and decide which are worth presenting to the whole class. Some selected sites are included at the end of this book though, as always with the internet, sites can change or even disappear. At least poetry readings don't go out of date or out of fashion.

Interesting as a recording might be, children will not necessarily engage with it unless there is some form of interaction. You might, therefore, try to find two (or more) recordings of the same poem and get them to discuss which they prefer and why.

It is also possible for you, as teacher or librarian, to make a recording. Again, you could read the poem in different ways, making varying use of emphases and pauses. Even better, get the headteacher to record a few poems. 'Do you recognise this voice?'

There are many video interpretations of Trevor's poem 'Sad I Ams' as a search on YouTube will reveal. They are of varying quality but they will give an idea of the many ways in which this approach can be used.

Making and using recordings

This might seem like a major undertaking but there are many very simple ways of tackling this kind of project, given the availability of technology. Laptops, tablets and mobile phones all have sound and

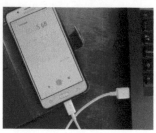

video apps built in. If you're not sure of how to operate them, young people will help! You can transfer recordings from a phone using Bluetooth or other synchronising methods but the most foolproof method is probably a simple cable, cheaply purchased online. Recording straight on to a laptop (or other computer) will allow you to play back the result immediately in a way which more children will be able to see or hear.

Don't underestimate the usefulness of sound recordings. For one thing they are easier to manage and edit than video and take up less space. Also, audio makes children concentrate on the words rather than on how they look!

A recording of a poem can be a solo enterprise or one undertaken by a small group, who can divide up the lines between them. It's worth rehearsing this and intervening with a bit of directing so that everyone is included. Slower or less confident readers can have shorter or easier lines and should be given time to practice before recording. In any event, recording can be done several times to get it right. Do make sure that children do not stop at the end of a line when the sense continues to the next one.

The recordings can then be played to the other groups to introduce a new poem or to interpret a familiar one. You could also have each group record a version of the same poem and then discuss the presentations. If the class is up for it, there could even be a competitive Great Sound-Off

'Voice recorder' is a basic app which should be already on your machine. If not, there will be something similar.

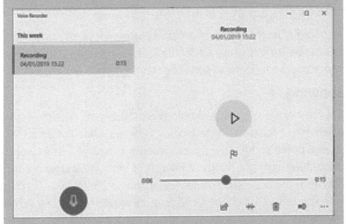

It's straightforward to record and save – and there is also a 'trim' function (third icon from the right) which, with a bit of care and practice you can use to delete ums and ers, coughs and too lengthy pauses.

>> Sad I Ams YouTube (or similar) videos?

11 How to make Technology work for you

Technology might not seem an ideal partner for poetry but it can, in fact, be an extremely useful tool. From the computer to the interactive whiteboard, all sorts of potential can be unlocked.

Showing

The most obvious use of technology is probably the data projector, whether or not it is connected to an interactive whiteboard. You can show a poem at the same time as reading it, enlarge certain words or phrases, highlight things of interest or difficulty and so on. You may also have access to internet resources which enable you to play video or sound clips of poems being read, sometimes accompanied by images. Some examples will be found at the end of this chapter with the usual caveat that web links can change or become broken.

If you are a PowerPoint user (or willing to become one) there are many opportunities to present poems in exciting ways though, as ever, don't let the bells and whistles overwhelm the content!

It's also a good way to show children's finished poems, though perhaps not as effective as…

Sharing

A child sharing something is likely to be more engaged than when he or she is just being shown something. Sharing children's work is difficult; simply reading it out doesn't allow much opportunity for feedback and discussion. An excellent low-tech solution to this is a device called a visualiser. It is, in essence, a camera on a stick and it takes whatever image it is focused on and shows it on a screen, or a blank wall.

One of the most effective things you can do when helping children with their writing is to model the writing process. Even better if you can use children's own writing to do this – with their permission, of course. During a writing session, select a piece of writing in process and put it under the visualiser so everyone can see.

Here is an opportunity to point out interesting words and phrases but also suggestions to be made, both by you and by the group. 'How about moving this line from here to here? Does anyone have an idea for how we could end this line? Tracy is trying to find a better word for….' And so on.

If you don't have a visualiser, you could use a camera and transfer the image to a laptop and thence to the screen. If you have everything set up ready, it only takes moments.

Creating

The humble computer is a perfect tool for drafting and reworking writing, especially poems. Why poems? Because they tend to be short and you can see all or most of them on screen at one time. Changing a word or words is easy – no crossing out, no insertion marks, asterisks and arrows. Moving a line or a group of lines can be time consuming and/or confusing on paper; on screen it's simplicity itself, especially if you use this short-cut in Word: position the cursor in the line you wish to move, hold down Shift and Alt and use the up / down arrow keys. Crucially, the facilities of the computer *allow* experimentation. Children can ask themselves, does this seem better or not? If not, Ctrl Z (or Undo) will put it back. You may need to demonstrate this powerful function for them to realise how liberating it is.

Another powerful technique to help children get started on some writing is to present them with a bank of words from which to draw. Rather than creating one yourself, why not take an existing poem and turn it into a rich source of ideas? On the next page, for example, are the words from Kit Wright's *Magic Box*, with duplicate words removed. We have utilised this with lots of children, with delightful results. The rules you apply are up to you. (We usually stipulate only these words can be used or, at most five extra words can be added.)

Why is this a use of technology? Firstly, because it works well if children have access to a computer and they can simply drag and drop words, just like fridge magnets! Though, printed out, it can also be used conventionally.

> a an ancient and are ashore Atlantic baby beach black blue box breakers broomstick Chinese colour corners cowboy dinosaurs dragon electric fifth fire first fish from gold great high-rolling hinges horse I ice in is its joints joke last leaping lid man my night nostrils of on put rumbling sari season secrets shall silk sip smile snow spark spoken stars steel summer sun surf swish the then three toe tongue tooth top touching uncle violet wash water white wild wishes witch with yellow

Secondly, unless you wish to type out the words yourself, it helps to use Word to create the word hoard. Instructions can be found at the back of this book, together with some examples of children's writing using this technique.

Investigating

Finally, a couple of ideas on how to use Word to get children to focus closely on the text, to look like a Scene of Crime detective at the words on the page.

Share a poem with the group so that they are a little familiar with it. Then de-sequence it and display it using a data projector and/ or interactive whiteboard. Can they put the lines back into the right order? What clues are there apart from making sense – verse pattern, rhyme scheme? Use the technique described above to move lines and try out different combinations.

A quick way to de-sequence a poem is, once you have it in Word, is to highlight the text and use the Sort button to put the lines into alphabetical order.

The poem does not have to be complex. Try this one:

And she was the Jersey cow
Because she knew not how
For he was only the farmer's boy
He lifted up the bars

She neither smiled nor thanked him
The sky was dotted with stars
They reached the gate together
They walked the lane together

Here is another way to intrigue children and get them to look closely at the words on the page – or, in this case, the words not on the page…

Select your poem and paste it into Word. Select the whole text and then go to Font Colour and choose white. The poem disappears. However, a double click anywhere in the poem will select a word and you can change the colour back to the original or use another colour entirely. Children are asked to predict the words that might come before or after the ones that have been revealed. Alternatively, you may choose to blank out certain words:

They		*the lane together*
The	*was dotted with stars*	
They		*the gate*
He	*up the bars*	
(etc.)		

There are many more ways in which simple applications such as Word can be utilised in a creative manner – and not just for poetry; (see *Improving Literacy with ICT*, Trevor Millum, Bloomsbury).

12 How to make the most of a Short Session: Reading

There's never enough time in the day – we all know that – but there's no need to neglect your poetic activities; you can use short sessions (10, 15, 30 minutes) to read, share, learn, appreciate and even write some poetry.

Reading/Sharing/Appreciating

There's an endless supply of poems that can be read in well under five minutes. When time is really tight you could read a poem to children, in a school or a library session, simply for pleasure and leave it at that. If there is time you could ask if the children have enjoyed the poem, what they liked about it, and, with a really short piece, you can easily examine it and look at how it's been constructed. It could be used, later, as a starting point for the children's own writing. What about this one:

Last night last night
I had a fright
I thought I saw a puma
Today today
It was all okay
I'd only seen a rumour

('Puma' by Trevor Millum
from *Double Talk*)

Read that aloud to the children a couple of times. Then show them what it looks like on the page. They'll be able to see that there's a lot going on, even in such a simple poem. Note the rhyme scheme it follows and mention the puma/rumour rhyme. Ask them to list other words that rhyme but don't share the same spelling e.g. hour flower, thumb glum, scheme dream. They could also suggest words (known as *homophones*) that sound identical but don't share the same spelling e.g. rain reign, too two, jeans genes, eight ate, wait weight. Not only will this help with improving spelling and increasing vocabulary, but it will also provide a word list which the children can make use of if they want to try their hand at a similar poem.

Here's a gentle six line poem that can be read aloud, without rushing it (including the title!) in just thirteen seconds.

> *Flake on flake*
> *the snow*
> *rewrites the garden.*
> *Word on word*
> *the poem*
> *settles on the page.*

('January Poem' by Catherine Benson from *Poetry Zone*)

As with 'Puma', read it aloud at least twice and then show the children what it looks like on the page. Read it again. Ask the children to close their eyes while they listen – to imagine snow falling on the garden and words floating down and settling on the page – allow them to really savour the words and the image. To help with their appreciation of the poem mention the clever positioning of *rewrites* and *settles*. In everyday conversation you'd be more likely to say that the poet *rewrites* a poem and that snow *settles* on the garden. Such attention to detail will benefit their own writing in the future.

One poem might well lead on to another. 'Puma' might encourage them to look for more animal poems. 'January Poem' could inspire them to find more poems about the seasons and the weather.

Having had sessions where you've provided the poem, ask the children to suggest suitable poems that the class can look at in future short sessions. Hopefully they'll get excited about becoming 'Poem Hunters.' They can bring their choices to you, in advance, so that you can copy, or type them up ready to look at on the white board, but let the child be the person who reads the poem aloud. If there are some children who prefer not to do this, rather than put them off looking for poems, let them know that you are willing to read it out or that they can nominate a friend to be the reader. You could ask them to look out for poems in their own time or devote a short session to looking through poetry books to see what they can find. The benefit here is that they will end up reading lots of poems regardless of whether they get used in class.

Off by Heart

Short poems, of course, are perfect for short sessions. A six-liner containing a few rhymes (such as 'Puma') can be easily memorised. It can live quietly in a child's head for the rest of the day. It can accompany them during breaks and over lunch. They can recite it to their family when they get home. They can be thinking about it as they fall asleep.

As grown-ups know, some poems, learnt as a child (and indeed when you're older), remain with you for the rest of your life. On dull grey days (or when he visits Huddersfield!) a line from 'Huddersfield', by Roger McGough, which describes the sky as being 'the colour of frozen lard', always creeps back into Bernard's mind. Having been introduced to 'January Poem' you'll probably be picturing snowflakes *rewriting* the garden many winters from now.

But there's no reason why longer poems shouldn't be made use of too. Trevor has had a class learn Auden's 'Night Mail.' They didn't have to learn the whole thing. Each child memorised only one line. They stayed at their desks and just went around the class in order, one voice following another. This was a Year 7 class so, below that age, we suggest just using the first section of the poem, which consists of sixteen rhythmical lines.

You could try the same method using Blake's 'The Tyger.' It has 24 lines but, as it's likely you will have more than 24 children in your class, some of the lines are suitable for splitting and sharing between two pupils:

> **And what shoulder,** *& what art*
> **What dread hand?** *& what dread feet?*
> **What the hammer?** *what the chain?*
> **What the anvil?** *what dead grasp*

(from 'The Tyger' by William Blake)

Another option is not to divide a poem up for individual voices but to learn a poem, as a class, over a series of short sessions. 'The Tyger' has six verses of four lines each so you could aim for at least one verse per session. You'll soon have a piece ready for performing.

A couple of modern poems we've heard classes perform recently are Roger McGough's 'The Sound Collector' and 'The Dragon Who Ate Our School' by Nick Toczek. A 'choir' of up to thirty voices reciting a poem in unison can sound fantastic. Bernard has had the surprise, and the pleasure, of hearing his own poem 'Ref Rap' coming back at him during his performance on a return visit to a school. He fell silent and left them to it when he heard the entire cohort of KS2 pupils joining in with

I don't win
I don't lose
I point the finger
Uphold the rules
I show the card
I send them off
I blow the whistle
When I've had enough

(from 'Ref Rap' by Bernard Young
in *What Are You Like?*)

There are lots of poems out there. Your 'Poem Hunters' will be able to discover many more to read, share, learn and perform. Just think of all those assemblies where your class will be able to shine. Happy hunting!

13 How to make the most of a Short Session: Writing

Here are some ideas (by no means an exhaustive list) suitable for short bursts of writing that can be returned to later.

5 Minute Exercise

Ask the children to write for three minutes. Tell them you'll time them. Once their pen/pencil touches the paper they must keep writing – they can write about anything that comes into their heads. It's more about quantity than quality at this stage and it doesn't  matter if it's messy as long as they can make sense of it later. Do let them know that you're not planning to look at their writing (unless they want you to). If anyone's stuck tell them to put 'As soon as I woke up this morning, I decided I'd…' and go from there. At the end of the 3 minutes tell them to stop and spend a couple of minutes looking over what they've written. They can circle any words or phrases that they think they might be able to develop at another time. Even if they don't produce anything of value this is still a useful exercise. It gets them writing and flexes the writing muscle.

Rhyming Couplets

Ask the children to work in pairs. Give each pair a short list of rhyming words e.g. *mad, bad, glad, sad, lad, dad* or *space, place, chase, case, face*. (You can easily find more by consulting a rhyming dictionary or by searching online – typing 'space rhymes' soon brings up a long list). It doesn't matter if some of the pairs have the same set of words. In fact, it's interesting to discover how similar or varied the results are. Ask them to write at least one rhyming couplet. Share some of the results. You might get

> *When I got home I didn't know why my Dad*
> *was standing there looking so mad.*

Lots of possibilities here. Why was dad mad? Is it because of something the writer has done? Has someone scraped his car? And what if 'sad' had been chosen instead of 'mad'? Maybe the dog has died. (Hope not!). The list of rhymes can now be ignored if they wish. The writers can continue the poem whenever time allows, using rhymes of their choosing. Continuing the poem using rhyming couplets means the form lends itself to adding at least a couple of lines at a sitting. Slowly, but surely, the poem will grow.

Steal

Well, let's say Borrow, a line or two from another poem. There are plenty to choose from. What about 'You can hear my knees are knocking' from Neal Zetter's poem 'Scared of the Dark' or 'There's a killer caterpillar on the loose!' from 'Killer Caterpillar' by Hilda Offen. We've found that 'After school what suits me' works well.

After school
what suits me
is to sit on the carpet
and watch TV.
Watch TV

Watch TV
I sit on the carpet
And watch TV.

(*See* Appendix *for the full poem*)

Who knows what will suit? Maybe

After school
what suits me
is to stand on my head
and count to three.
Count to three

Count to three
I stand on my head
and count to three.

Or, changing it slightly (there's no law that says you have to stick rigidly to the 'borrowed' text) - 'When I get home/what I like to do/is write a poem/that sounds as if it's true.' That could be the whole poem or the beginning of a poem with a pattern that can be returned to and added to in another short session.

For Sale/Career Opportunity

In class take a look at some 'small ads' which can be found in newspapers, magazines and online. Pay attention to the wording. Ask them to think of something unusual to sell – their school, a library, a poet, a baby brother! Get them to list some things that would encourage someone to buy the item. It's a good idea to work through an example with the children before they write their own.

> *Very low mileage brother. As eco-*
> *Nomical as any other. Must mention*
> *Does need some attention. Stream-*
> *Lined, rear spoiler. Runs on milk,*
> *baby oil and gripe water. Serviced -*
> *Needs rear wash/wipe. Only one*
> *Owner - not yet run in. Will swap*
> *For anything!*

(*See* Appendix *for the full poem*)

A similar idea is to take a look at job adverts. Then list some out-of-the-ordinary jobs/careers (wizard, witch, footballer, prince/princess, Dr Who!) Consider the skills/qualities required to do that job. Bernard loved stories about King Arthur and knights in shining armour when he was a boy.

> *Are you courageous, honourable*
> *and chivalrous?*
> *Do you like wearing metal suits*
> *and enjoy being called Sir?*
> *Then this could be the job for you.*

(*See* Appendix *for the full poem*)

What does it take to be a witch? Must you hate children and be wicked? What does a witch eat? What do they wear?

Are you wicked, ghastly, gruesome?
Do you hate all children
and love to wear black?
Do you go out in a pointy hat
and eat frog's eyes on toast
when you fancy a snack?
Then this could be the job for you.

Become an Animal!

Choose an animal you'd like to be. Snake, lion, parrot, dog, cat? Jot down some facts about the animal you've chosen so that you've got something to refer to. Begin your poem with 'I'm a …' and become that animal.

I'm a cat
an ordinary cat
it's so simple
simple as that

Yes, I'm a cat
an ordinary cat
and I do what cats do

I like to stare
and drink from a tap
I like to purr
when I'm sitting on a lap

I use my litter
when I need to poo
I do what cats do

(*See* Appendix *for the full poem*)

You could apply this to being a person. Imagine what it would be like to be in someone else's shoes (or space-boots!). 'I'm a spacewoman…' 'I'm the King…' 'I'm that person you see sleeping in a doorway…' 'I'm the man in the moon…'

You could write as if you're an object. You could be a mobile phone, a TV set, a guitar, someone's hat or a very odd sock.

Class Poems

Class poems have been covered in the 'How to get them started writing a poem' chapter but it's worth mentioning here that, in our experience, it's possible (and great fun) to create a group poem in under 30 minutes. It can be revisited in other short sessions where it can be edited and rehearsed.

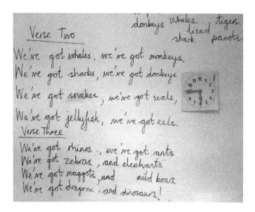

14 How to read a poem aloud

Some of us are happy to perform, some of us would rather stay in the shadows. Reading aloud is a fairly safe option for those who are not natural performers. However, a poem can be read well or badly and it is worth taking the trouble to do it well as it is one of the best ways for children to encounter poetry.

Usually, you will know in advance which poem you will be reading. Occasionally you may happen upon a poem in the course of a session and want to share it or you may be asked to read a child's own poem out to the group. Mostly, though, you will have time to prepare and, even if you only spend five minutes doing so, it's worth it.

When you first read the poem through look out for any trips and hazards. These might be tricky or unfamiliar words or unusual word order. Take, for example, the third verse of 'Daffodils'.

> *The waves beside them danced; but they*
> *Out-did the sparkling waves in glee:*
> *A poet could not but be gay,*
> *In such a jocund company:*
> *I gazed—and gazed—but little thought*
> *What wealth the show to me had brought:*

The last line would normally be expressed as 'What wealth the show had brought to me' but the poet wants to rhyme brought and thought and so, as often happens, has carried out a little trick with the word order. If you're aware of it, you will be able to read the lines smoothly and with the right stress. (You might also want to be ready for 'jocund', meaning merry.)

In Masefield's 'Cargoes', there are a number of unfamiliar words and part of the pleasure of the poem lies in relishing them. But you will want to decide beforehand quite how to say 'quinquereme, Nineveh and Ophir', not to mention 'Isthmus, amethysts and moidores'!

Another thing to be aware of is the 'run-on line' or 'enjambement' as some like to call it. Reading the verse from 'Daffodils', you can pause slightly at the end of most lines but if you do so at the end of the first line it will sound awkward, so you must read 'but they out-did the sparkling waves in glee' in one go. The same is true of the first two lines of the poem and the first four lines of the second verse.

If children have a copy of the poem in front of them, one reading might be enough, but with poems of the length of 'Daffodils' and 'Cargoes' two readings would probably be better.

'Performing' a poem is not much more than reading it aloud with extra energy and expression. Some poems lend themselves to performance, others less so. 'Daffodils' would not be an obvious choice to perform, whereas 'Cargoes' could benefit from a changing tempo. The first verse would be read slowly, lazily almost; the second slightly faster and the final verse at a cracking pace. See 'How to help children perform'.

Let's look at a well-known poem and see how you might annotate it in preparation for a reading.

'The Listeners' by Walter de la Mare

'Is there anybody there?' said the Traveller,	Louder for the voice of the Traveller.
Knocking on the moonlit door;	
And his horse in the silence champed the grasses	Knock on table / desk.
Of the forest's ferny floor:	Fairly quiet.
And a bird flew up out of the turret,	
Above the Traveller's head:	
And he smote upon the door again a second time;	Loud knock on table.
'Is there anybody there?' he said.	Loud but not a shout.
But no one descended to the Traveller;	
No head from the leaf-fringed sill	
Leaned over and looked into his grey eyes,	
Where he stood perplexed and still.	
But only a host of phantom listeners	Pause.
That dwelt in the lone house then	
Stood listening in the quiet of the moonlight	As quiet as possible while still audible.
To that voice from the world of men:	

Stood thronging the faint moonbeams on the
dark stair,
  That goes down to the empty hall,
Hearkening in an air stirred and shaken
  By the lonely Traveller's call.
And he felt in his heart their strangeness,   Returning to normal
  Their stillness answering his cry,   volume.
While his horse moved, cropping the dark turf,
  'Neath the starred and leafy sky;
For he suddenly smote on the door, even   A really loud knocking.
  Louder, and lifted his head:—
'Tell them I came, and no one answered,   A frustrated shout.
  That I kept my word,' he said.
Never the least stir made the listeners,
  Though every word he spake
Fell echoing through the shadowiness of the
still house
  From the one man left awake: Getting quieter.
Ay, they heard his foot upon the stirrup,
  And the sound of iron on stone,
And how the silence surged softly backward,   Down to a whisper.
  When the plunging hoofs were gone.

However, you approach the poems you are going to read, give
them proper attention. Even a limerick deserves to be read well, and
a haiku even more so!

15 How to help children perform

There are all sorts of occasions when you might want to have poems read aloud – and not by you. Perhaps at the beginning of a session to introduce a poem or a theme; or within a writing activity to share ways of tackling a task or to share work at the end of a session. It might be that, while children are writing, you notice an interesting piece and want to use it as an example. 'This is a poem that's not finished but it might give you an idea of how to tackle this topic / theme / subject…'

As well as readings that take place during a session, there are also occasions where more formal presentations or performances take place: school assembly, for example.

Some children can't wait to read out loud, others are extremely reticent. Those who are willing are not always the best writers or, indeed, the best readers. There are a number of reasons to encourage children reading aloud:

- if it is their work, it gives the writing status;
- it makes them focus on a text in a different way;
- it enables immediate feedback;
- and simply, it enables sharing.

Whether the reader is confident or shy, there are ways to improve reading aloud.

Volume

Volume is often a problem. Those whose voices are very clear and loud in the playground are often the ones who are most quiet when speaking in class. When only the front row can hear what is being said, you need to take action. Go to the back of the room and ask the child to speak to you. We have often gone even further and stepped outside the door, saying 'We want to hear you out here!' This extreme approach seems to work.

Speed

A common problem is that of children reading far too fast, usually when it is their own work. Perhaps they want to get it over with or, because the words are familiar to them and they don't yet have an appreciation of their audience. Merely saying 'slow down' isn't very effective so you may have to adopt other strategies.

Mark the piece to be read (or better still, get the writer to do so) where pauses can be inserted. We tend to use a single forward slash / for a short pause and a double // for a longer one. You may need to instruct the reader to count 'one' or 'one, two' when meeting these marks and practise it a few times. This could also be a whole group activity. Sometimes the pause will be at the end of a line but not always. If it is a 'run on' line, make sure the reader does go on without a pause! Most (but not all) poems are punctuated like prose and those marks need to be attended to.

You could also record the same poems read at different speeds and ask the group to say which ones work best. At the same time, point out how important a pause can be in gaining the audience's attention.

Posture

Most reading aloud will be done standing up – though if you have a high stool, like a lab or bar stool, that can work well and establish a less formal feeling. A lectern or music stand is a handy thing to have available, given that a floppy piece of paper is not easy to read from and frequently gets held in front of the reader's face. Fix it to the music stand with a bulldog clip or a peg: you'll be surprised at the difference it makes. All this contributes to the reader being able to concentrate more on standing up straight and projecting his or her voice.

If children are reading from a book, the print should be fairly clear but if they are reading their own work, it might be helpful for them to write out a larger copy. If you are preparing a performance, it's worth having the poems typed up and printed out in a clear font.

Actions and facial expression can of course be added for greater effect, if the poem is suitable. The second verse of Trevor's poem 'Exploding Heads' with opportunities for pulling faces and knocking knees is a good example.

> *He was in a state*
> *In a terrible tizz*
> *His eyes were rotating*
> *And his tongue, it went FIZZ.*
> *His knees started knocking*
> *Made a terrible row*
> *And then – he blew up*
> *With a furious KAPOW!*

(from *Too Much Schooling Can Damage Your Health*)

However, do not be tempted into overacting – the most effective part of a performance is the voice. Whether slow or fast, high or low, keep it clear so that the audience can hear every syllable.

See also: How to put on a Performance

Here's an extract from a poem by Coral Rumble where we have suggested pause marks:

> *When my dad watches the news…/*
> *You can start lots of fights*
> *And swing from the lights,/*
> *You can throw all the cushions about,//*
> *You can smash every plate,/*
> *Keep on slamming the gate*
> *And wear all your clothes inside out;//*

(from 'When my Dad watches the news' in *Unzip your Lips Again*)

Note: we always make a point of asking permission from the writer before reading out his or her work. It's a matter of courtesy.

16 How to put on a performance

One of the things guaranteed to get children engaging with poetry is a performance. It will engage both the performers and the audience.

What to perform

It's your choice whether children perform poems they have written or published ones that they like and have chosen. Indeed, it could be a mixture, which gives status to their own writing when showcased alongside that of well-known poets.

Obviously, some poems are more suited to public performance than others. A quiet, reflective poem is more difficult to present than a poem with a strong rhythm and rhyme – and which might also have amusing content as well. Think, though, about the performance as a whole. It's good to aim for a variety of content and of style. You will also want to balance strong performers with weak ones, solo performers with pairs or groups.

How to perform

We have used the term 'perform' to cover both reading from a script and reciting a poem that has been learnt by heart. If you are short of time, reading poems is quite acceptable. However, learning to read from a script is not simple and children will need to practise the way they hold their text and how they view it. A good half-way-house is for children to learn their poems but have the text with them 'just in case'. It is also better to use a lectern / music stand than to hold a piece of paper and on a practical note, having three stands at different heights available is better than having to adjust the height for each child!

Children like to perform in pairs or small groups. It's a good exercise in sharing and co-operation as well as helping to understand the poem which is to be divided up between different voices. Any more than three voices can be difficult to choreograph, though, and even two or three children performing together needs careful thought and preparation. Without it, there will be mix ups, nudges and whispers of 'it's your turn!'

Rehearsing a performance, however brief it may be, or however small or familiar the audience, makes an enormous difference. Make the most of any breaks or playtimes to suggest pairs or groups practise, practise, practise. Individuals will also benefit from trying out their reading with a friend. Do 'quality assure' the final version of anything to be performed, though; it's not that you don't trust them, it's that you are the producer / director and, in the end, it's your show and you want them to be a credit to themselves and to you.

See also How to help children perform *for further tips.*

When to perform – and to whom?

Trevor and Bernard have both put on performances at the end of a single day's session. Poems have been written, edited and rehearsed all in one day, ready for a show for parents at three o'clock. This has the merit of keeping things fresh and lively and instils a sense of urgency (if not panic).

However, it is unlikely that you will have the luxury of a whole day with one group, so a more relaxed approach can be taken. The most obvious occasions to stage a performance are in a scheduled school assembly or at the end of the day for parents or other visitors. Sharing children's work with the class or group is good, sharing it with the school is better, sharing it with the wider world of parents and grandparents is best!

As a further step, poems can be performed in an even more public way as part of a concert or in the interval of a play. Even an in-school performance can be enhanced by some publicity.

New Poems by Y5

Thursday Assembly

 Don't miss it!

Finally

Putting on a poetry performance raises the status of poetry and gives children an opportunity to stand up in public. Start as young as possible so that it never becomes frightening. Shy children can be introduced to public performance gradually. They can be part of a group or they can read from a script – and they can be guided to perform something which suits their personality.

We remember one rather diffident girl who chose a short but 'difficult' poem ('He Wishes for the Cloths of Heaven' by W B Yeats) and read it slowly and clearly, sitting on a tall stool, lit by a single spotlight. She was surprised at how powerful this turned out to be and by the praise she received.

Further hints and tips

Poetry by Heart is a national competition for older students but its website has some very good advice on improving the public presentation of poems. See the 'teach' section in particular and, within that, 'Poetry's Four Dimensions' is especially helpful, whether children are performing existing poems or their own. poetrybyheart.org.uk/learningzone/teach/

17 How to 'Publish'

Publication is a great motivator. Having your work 'out there' for people to read other than your teacher, parents or grandparents is a good feeling. It means your work is being taken seriously. It also focuses attention on quality and, of course, on whom we see as the audience.

Many years ago, Trevor collected stories and poems from his two Y9 classes, typed them up and turned them into a duplicated booklet which he gave out to mums and dads on Parents' Evening. He was surprised at the reaction of both children and parents. 'It was such a simple thing but they were really pleased – and surprised.' Part of the surprise was that someone had taken the time and trouble to produce the booklet but it was also the delight of seeing one's work in print.

This is still true even in a world of digital media. The printed word has a status above that of words on a screen – perhaps it is undeserved but nevertheless it seems to hold true. That's not to say you shouldn't use newer methods of publishing, though. Poetry lends itself to a wide range of publishing possibilities…

Print

The prevalence of photocopiers and scanners make the creation of publication on paper very much easier than it was when Trevor was making his booklets. But even without any technology children's work can be 'published' on notice boards in a classroom, library and around the building. The wider the audience, the greater the sense of satisfaction! At the simplest level, poems can be written out (and, inevitably, decorated or illustrated), mounted and fixed to any notice board. Poems are usually quite short so make sure the WRITING IS BIG and CLEAR!

The computer adds another dimension, of course, with its ability to present different fonts, colours and sizes. However, do not let children play with these until the poem is written – it is such a distraction. It can be used as a motivator, though. 'When we're satisfied that the poem is the best possible one, then you can type it up – any way you like.'

Once you have a single, good copy, whether handwritten or typed, a booklet is an option. This takes more work and children will understand it is a special thing to do – so there are additional responsibilities regarding carefully crafted writing and proof-reading. Involve children in the editorial process. Perhaps there are choices to be made about which poems to include. Everyone should have the opportunity to be included, of course, but which of X or Y's poems is better – and what is the best order for the poems in the booklet?

It is possible for this to be a group activity. Each table of six or seven could produce its own mini-booklet, with all the decisions delegated to the group. This kind of work necessitates a wide range of skills including reading, decision making, sharing, discussion and working to a deadline.

Let's not forget the option of individual little booklets. An A4 sheet can be made into an A7 (7 x 10.5cm) booklet of 8 sides; A3 will produce handy A6 pages. Here's how:

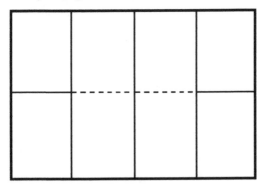

Fold the paper in half, then half again and again so that you have eight rectangles. Cut along the middle (the dotted line), fold lengthways and then push the two ends together.

Children can either write directly onto the pages or, our preferred method, cut and paste (with real scissors and glue). The advantage of the latter, though messier, is that a mistake can be rectified. It's so disappointing to make a big error on the seventh page of your carefully written booklet of poems.

Digital

The most straightforward way of publishing digitally is to put children's work on the school or library website. If the website does not have a special place for children's work – shame! Once established, it can be a brilliant showcase and, moreover, easily updated.

There are also internet sites which will publish children's work, too. We recommend the *Poetry Zone* created and run by our own Roger Stevens poetryzone.co.uk but you will find others (mainly in the USA) with a web search.

We hesitate to mention PowerPoint or similar presentation software because they can be 'time vampires'. However, now and then, as a special project, turning a poem into a PowerPoint presentation can be very effective. A sequence of these showing on a loop during breaks or Parents' Evenings make a great showcase. Again, poems are generally short, so they can be taken in and appreciated in a way that a story, for example, cannot.

Painting and drawing applications can, like PowerPoint, make a short piece of writing very powerful. For children who do not write much of any length, this can be a boost to their self-esteem. We're reminded of a child who wrote 'the hawk circles in the sky like a carousel'. It's a perfect image but she felt it didn't make a poem. Using the basic application Paint, she made it into something quite different. This mono reproduction doesn't have the zing of the original one in blues and greens, but you get the idea.

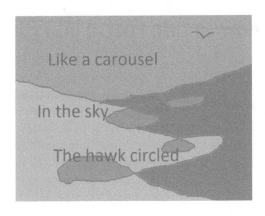

Notice, we decided that the poem had more impact if we moved the hawk to the last line. In a later, PowerPoint version we made the lines appear one by one and appear in a twirling motion. Result: one very happy poet.

18 How to turn Poetry into Funetry

As you will have realised by now, poetry leaves a lot of room for fun. Children are actively encouraged to play with words. Puns, double meaning or ambiguities are all part of the poet's craft. Think what fun you can have with sound: rhythm and rhyme appeal to all children and if too much alliteration turns into tongue-twisters, just enjoy it. Apart from sound, there's the satisfaction to be had from the unconventional layout of words on the page: look up Edwin Morgan and Dylan Thomas or research 'shape poems'.

Here are a few suggestions for taking the 'po-face' out of poetry and replacing it with fun – or perhaps, beyond fun to challenging, unusual, intriguing…

Where poems might be found and how they might be displayed

It's nice for a school or library to have a poetry wall or notice-board; however, why not write poems on a till roll and stretch it along a corridor or around a room?

Put the words of a poem in bold writing on separate post-its so that children can rearrange them. This is like fridge magnets without the need for magnets – or a fridge. They won't last so long but that doesn't matter. You can photograph the post-it poem if you want to keep a record.

Write a poem in chalk on the playground.

Create a PowerPoint display on a loop.

A widely used idea but very simple and attractive: peg 'word-cards' on a line across the room or better still, across a corridor or other more widely used space.

Here's a challenge. Find or write a poem that has the same number of words as the children in the class or group. Write each word on an A4 piece of paper or card. Children get into a huddle and then see how quickly they can arrange the poem. Take a photo. Now see if you can rearrange the poem and still make sense; sometimes something quite interesting results.

If you haven't come across them before, 'word clouds' are great fun and quite addictive. There are a number of different word cloud generators on-line and this site reviews several:

blog.polleverywhere.com/best-word-cloud-generator/

This example, using the words from 'Ten Little Schoolchildren' uses an app called Worditout (worditout.com)

Most of the word cloud generators will vary the size of a word depending on how frequently it appears in the text, while removing words such as 'and' and 'the'. This can be a useful way into examining word choice in different texts, not just in poetry.

After Christmas collage: children bring Christmas cards and cut or tear out the words. Arrange them into adjectives, verbs and nouns (who said SPAG couldn't be fun?) and then pin them to a pin board so that you get a huge message. Better still, save them for next December.

wishing hoping **have a**
MERRY happy peaceful **new**
all the best
XMAS **SEASON** yule
year winter **wish**

Creating poems in different ways

Collage

That last idea (which can be applied to other kinds of cards of course) brings us to ways of creating or finding poems. The technique of creating a collage of words can be applied to other sources. Labels from food and drink containers are rich in interesting language: just read the back of a crisp packet.

Found poems

If you have a rich enough piece of prose, a 'found poem' can often be quarried from it. The following words are taken from two paragraphs of Chapter Three of *The Secret Garden*.

> no more questions
> darkness
> glimpses of odd things
> hedges and trees.
> a long time
> a long time
> no more hedges
> and no more trees
> nothing
> but a dense darkness
> great expanse of dark
> a wind rising
> a wild, low, rushing sound
> darkness
> no more questions

The last two lines have been taken from the beginning and repeated. Otherwise all the words are in the same order as they appear in the story. (Lines can be reordered if you wish, and – reminder - a simple way to do that in Word is to use Shift + Alt and the up/down arrow keys.) The choice of words is key and it makes a good group activity for children to suggest words and phrases while you highlight them on an interactive whiteboard.

Nonsense Poems

Nonsense poems are nothing of the sort, of course. If a poem was completely nonsensical, we wouldn't bother to try to read it. Edward Lear or Spike Milligan might be thought of as writers of Nonsense poems but the words always make sense in some way – and, moreover, the syntax works. Even in a phrase such as

'The warg moodled the flipsy bidger'

everyone knows that moodled is a verb, flipsy an adjective and so on. 'Bidger warg flipsy moodled the' would indeed be nonsense and no one would be interested.

Lewis Carroll's 'Jabberwocky' famously invents words without ever causing the reader to wonder what is going on. Roald Dahl was also a great creator of new words (or neologisms). The trick is to create the new word in a way that enables the reader to feel it fits. If you want to try creating new words, it's best to start with an existing poem. How about 'Daffodils'?

I phooted lonely as a snurl
That flibs on high o'er flurps and flimps,
When all at once I saw a gharl,
A gruggle, of grossiful grizzilimps.

Alliteration and rhyme become easy, don't they? But children still need to pay attention to the rhythm and stress of the lines. There can also be some discussion of why some words are easier to replace than others. Words such as 'on', 'of' and 'at', for example; so small yet so important!

Once you start thinking outside the box page, all sorts of ideas may occur to you – and to children you work with. Go with it.

19 How to get the best from a visiting poet

Arranging the visit

We'll give you information about how and where to find poets in the Appendix but, for now, let's agree that you've decided who you think is the right poet for you. A good start is to email them and ask what availability they have, what they charge, what they can offer.

Try to identify your aims and let the poet know what you're hoping for. Do you want a performance to the whole school? Do you want workshops? Do you want the poet to visit classrooms and read some poems, to talk about writing and being a poet, to answer questions? Are you seeking to increase enthusiasm for reading and writing poetry?

Once that's sorted you need to agree on a timetable.

Timetable

If it's your first time organising a visit your poet will be able to suggest what works best and to offer a few alternatives as to how the day can be successfully timetabled. For a full day in a primary school we suggest a performance of about 30 minutes to the whole school at the start of the day (if you're a large primary school you can have a separate performance for each KS) followed by workshops.

As well as being a fun way to kick off the visit, the performance is an opportunity for the poet to say hello to everyone they'll be working with, and it's a time-saver – it gets the ball rolling and effortlessly generates ideas that the children can make use of in the workshops. We've had children come to us after a performance to say that they've already got poems started, and on occasions completed, in their heads after being inspired by what they heard.

Some poets are very specific about what ages they will work with, how long a workshop must be and how many children per session. Others will try and fit in with what you require. Ideally a workshop would last an hour and involve one class of about 30 children but we appreciate that many of you will want to give every child in your school the opportunity to work with a 'real live poet' and you can get good results in shorter sessions and even when the poet works with a couple of classes at a time. (It is possible to create presentable class poems in only 30 minutes which can then be performed to other classes. See the chapter on 'How to make the most of a short session').

Preparation

Show the children that you're getting excited about the visit. It's a good idea to look at some of the poet's poems before the day arrives. If you've no access to their books (some of their books may have gone out of print, some are published by small-scale publishers and not always easy to obtain) you're likely to find examples of their work on their website. There may well be recordings of them reading poetry, and videos and printed poems – all available for free. You can see what they look like and sound like and gather some autobiographical information.

The children might like to ask some questions and, when time allows, a good opportunity is near the end of the workshop. Get the children to prepare some questions – ideally not 'how old are you?' or 'how much do you earn?' (someone always asks that one!) but more along the lines of 'what made you want to be a poet?' 'where do you write?''how many poems have you written?''do you enjoy being a poet?' etc. And if anyone can come up with a really unusual question that makes it more interesting for everyone. There have been occasions when there hasn't been time for questions and we've taken the written ones away with us and answered them later by email.

Near to the visit

Contact them just to check that they're ready for the visit. Let them know where they can park, if they're coming by car, and if lunch will be provided. It's as well to have their mobile number too. And do let them know if you've needed to make any amendments to the timetable. Any changes shouldn't be a problem; just like you, experienced poets are used to thinking on their feet and being flexible and adapting to what happens on the day.

On the day

Don't leave your visitor hanging about in the entrance too long. They won't expect to be treated like royalty but they might have had a very early start, and travelled a fair distance, so will be in need of a hot drink and a visit to the toilet. A warm welcome goes a long way and sets the tone for the rest of the day.

Don't do your marking when the poet is performing. Let the children see that you're interested in what's going on.

Do make notes. The poet is likely to throw out lots of ideas that won't all get used on the day. You'll be able to gather them up and make use of them in the future.

Finally: Why Book A Poet?

You're giving the children the experience of meeting the person behind the words – perhaps someone just like them, who, at an early age, began to enjoy experimenting with words and learning how to express themselves. They'll be able to see that the poet is an ordinary person, most likely someone who did another job (lots of poets who write for children were teachers - Trevor was, Bernard was a librarian) before they discovered it was actually possible to earn a living as a writer. And, most importantly, a visiting poet can create a lasting impression on pupils.

Here's some feedback that we've received:

'Just wanted to a say a big thank you for organising the poet visit and the interactive sessions. Both my kids have been so inspired by him and poetry isn't something we or they have read much of – so it has been great to show them how poetry can work. Lucy has read every poem to us out of the book she bought and loves the fact that it has been signed by him especially for her. Really lovely to see them so excited about it.' – Parent

'Many thanks to you for a fabulous poetry morning! The children loved it and you have certainly inspired us adults with ideas to move our poetry topic along. It really was a very enjoyable morning and I will be recommending you to the rest of school so hopefully we will see you again!' – KS1 Teacher

'Just wanted to say thank you for the performances and workshops that you delivered. You really helped launch our Poetry Week and the children have produced some fantastic writing. They haven't stopped talking about it.' – Head Teacher

20 How to help children to carry on writing on their own

Your poetry work might well result in one or two children catching the writing bug and having the desire to do more. As a teacher or librarian, you're in a position to assist and encourage this process. But it will involve extra work for you and you'll need to have a love of poetry yourself if you're to show enthusiasm and interest in what they're doing. (We're assuming that if you're reading this book then you are that person). You can help them to develop as poets and writing poetry (and/or prose) might be something they will continue to do for the rest of their lives. Who knows, they might end up doing it as a job. It does happen!

Therefore, the purpose of this chapter is to offer some tips and advice that can be passed on to budding poets.

Things you can do

Read their work and offer constructive criticism.

Ensure they have access to poetry books so that they can broaden their reading of poetry and become familiar with the work of a variety of poets.

Look for ways to publish their work in your school or library and through publications and competitions. (Note: competitions may not be right for every child. If they don't win, they might be put off from further writing). *See useful addresses at the back of the book.*

Set them tasks that they're willing to do in their own time (as opposed to homework which they're obliged to do). If they really are that keen, and the task is enjoyable, they'll do it. There are plenty of writing exercises included in previous chapters.

Tips for you to pass on to children

Keep a notebook

As any writer will tell you, maintaining a notebook is essential. It's a place to keep a record of things you see and hear. A line from a poem or a song, or even an advert, might trigger a new poem, so jot it down before you forget. You might catch a bit of someone else's conversation or see something on TV. Once, when driving to the dentist, Bernard had the radio on. There was an item on the news about car thefts and burglaries and he heard the words 'a one man walking crime wave' being used. He liked the sound of that line and, appropriately, decided to steal it. It became the opening of a poem entitled 'Criminal':

I'm a one man
walking crime wave
Nothing you've got
is safe

Not your car Not your house
Not your money
Not your dreams Not your life
Not your grave

He's crooked
Proud of it

The crime rate soars
Goes through the roof
And I'm responsible
That's the truth

He's a villain
Makes a killing

(from 'Criminal' by Bernard Young in *What Are You Like?*)

Do get into the habit of making a note of anything you come across that might serve as the ingredients for a poem. Trevor, idly reading a chocolate biscuit wrapper, decided to note down its ingredients (which included emulsifier E322, milk chocolate flavouring, colouring 110,102,150, anti-oxidant 320 and salt!). Later, when he returned to his notebook and reread the ingredients list, he was inspired to write 'E322 – or Is my mother trying to kill me?' Usually mum packs healthy food…

But today she put a biscuit
In with all my grub
A chocolate covered biscuit
A symbol of her love
I idly read the packet
Saw what they put inside
I read the wrapper one more time
And then I nearly died!

(See Appendix *for the full poem*)

Once the notebook begins to fill up it becomes the raw material, the source, for further writing. Your keen writers may still welcome some input from you in the form of set tasks but they will, in time, get used to raiding their notebooks when they're in the mood to write and have less need for prompts.

Writing Tips

Dreams – Write them down when you wake up as they're often soon forgotten once the day gets going. You might dream that you're on a bus and suddenly it's a spaceship or a submarine. Think of what an exciting poem that could be. Your dreams might reflect some problem or issue that's troubling you. Writing about such things often helps. You don't have to show the poem to anyone if it's too personal.

Daydream – See what comes into your head. Jot down any interesting words, ideas, subjects, nonsense. A daydream can lead you anywhere. You could write a poem about something you would like to happen. You might find you end up thinking about real things that are going on in your life as well as the magical and fantastical.

Drift off
during your tea.
Don't watch TV. Tune in
to the pictures inside your head.
Have fun.

(from 'The School for Daydreamers' by Bernard Young in *What Are You Like?*)

Favourite Things – List things that you enjoy. You could write some cheerful, celebratory poetry that will do everyone good. Write about scoring the winning goal, making your mum smile, being welcomed home by your new puppy!

Unfavourite Things – Go on, have a grumble. What annoys you – having to go to bed too early (even though you know sleep is good for you), having to come offline when tea's ready, your little (or big) brother (or sister), your teacher, being told what to write your poems about!

Use your memories – Recall some memorable moments. Perhaps that day when you managed to do something you thought was impossible. Maybe there's a really embarrassing but, when you look back at it, very funny moment that occurred when you were with your friends or family. You could describe it but also write about how you were feeling. There will be times when you've felt elated but others where you've been sad. Try writing a poem that expresses such feelings. We all experience them and it will be something your readers can identify with. Your poem might make someone feel less alone.

What else can you write about – a favourite colour, swimming, dancing, shopping, ice cream, chocolate cake, cheese, friendship, arguments, having the flu, building a snowman, being stuck in a traffic jam, birthdays, Christmas, giggling, robots, robots giggling, football, space, falling asleep…

The fact is, poems can be about absolutely anything and there isn't space here to list everything. (And even if we tried to there would still be 'something' missing!)

Less is more – You'll often hear this said in writing workshops but do remember it. Poems are often short and can say things, things that are funny, serious things, in a quick way.

Show not tell – You'll quite often hear this said too. The idea is to give your reader clues as to what's happening or how someone's feeling. Writing 'I'm feeling fed up today' leaves nothing to the imagination and conveys no emotion.

Feelings?

I don't talk about them.

*I write down how I'm feeling
in my Feelings Diary.*

That helps.

*And when I'm fine
I don't write a line.*

My diary's almost full.

('Feelings' by Bernard Young in *What Are You Like?*)

Dear Teacher/Librarian

We hope this chapter will assist you in helping those individuals you encounter who, at a young age, begin to take their writing seriously. You might even get a mention when they become rich and famous!

One morning, having signed in at the school office, Bernard was waiting in the entrance to meet the teacher who'd arranged his visit.

A woman who'd just come in said, 'Hey, are you that poet who was here last year?'

'Er, yes I am,' said Bernard, wondering what sort of trouble he was in.

'Thought so,' she said. 'Well, my son hasn't stopped writing poetry since then.'

He's still not sure if that was a compliment or a complaint!

Appendix 1
Poems by Trevor and Bernard referred to in the book

Ten little schoolchildren

Ten little schoolchildren
Standing in a line.
One opened her mouth too far
And then there were nine.

Nine little schoolchildren
Trying not to be late.
One missed the school bus
And then there were eight.

Eight little schoolchildren
In the second eleven.
One twisted an ankle
And then there were seven.

Seven little schoolchildren
Trying out some tricks.
One went a bit too far
And then there were six.

Six little schoolchildren
Hoping teacher won't arrive.
One flicked a paper dart
And then there were five.

Five little schoolchildren
Standing by the door.
One tripped the teacher up
And then there were four.

Four little schoolchildren
Longing for their tea.
One was kept in after school
And then there were three.

Three little schoolchildren
Lurking by the loo.
Teacher saw a puff of smoke
And then there were two.

Two little schoolchildren
Think that fights are fun.
One got a bloody nose
And then there was one.

One little schoolchild
Playing in the sun.
Whistle blew, buzzer went,
Then there were none!

The Dark Avenger

My dog is called The Dark Avenger
Hello, I'm Cuddles

She understands every word I say
Woof?

Last night I took her for a walk
Woof! Walkies! Let's go!

Cleverly, she kept 3 paces ahead
I dragged him along behind me

She paused at every danger,
spying out the land
I stopped at every lamp-post

When the coast was clear, she
sped on
I slipped my lead and ran away

Scenting danger, Avenger
investigated
I found some fresh chip papers in the bushes

I followed, every sense alert
He blundered through the trees, shouting 'Oy, Come 'ere! Where are you?'

Something - maybe a sixth sense –
 told me to stop
He tripped over me in the dark

There was a pale menacing figure
ahead of us
*Then I saw the white Scottie from
next door*

Avenger sprang into battle, eager
to defend her master
Never could stand terriers

They fought like tigers
We scrapped like dogs

Until the enemy was defeated
*Till Scottie's owner pulled him off –
spoil sport!*

Avenger gave a victory salute
I rolled in the puddles

And came to check I was all right
I shook mud over him

'Stop it, you stupid dog!'
He congratulated me

Sometimes, even The Dark Avenger
can go too far.
Woof!!

E322
- or is my mother trying to kill me?

I don't have school dinners
My mum packs up a box

So I scoff my sarnies in the hall
Watch the others getting spots
I have brown bread with bits in
Spread with soya marge and cheese
I just stare at chips and custard
The batter and the peas
I get a balanced diet
Don't stuff myself with starch

Protect my teeth from sugar
Keep them strong and sharp
But today she put a biscuit
In with all my grub
A chocolate covered biscuit
A symbol of her love
I idly read the packet
Saw what they put inside
I read the wrapper once more time
And then I nearly died!
*There's
emulsifier E322
the sugar and the flour
whey powder, glucose syrup,
colouring (110, 102,150) and some
malt,
cocoa - fat reduced -
milk chocolate flavouring
(would you believe?)
anti-oxidant 320
and a little pinch of salt!*

I read it through just one more time
I gulped and then I thought
She's trying to kill me
　　But
　　　　I ate it anyway and
　　　　I'm not
　　　　　　Dead

Swap? Sell? Small Ads Sell Fast!

1990 Dad. Good runner– needs
one or
Two repairs – a few grey hairs but
Nothing a respray couldn't fix.
Would like a 1986 5-speed turbo
In exchange: something in the sporty
Twin-carb range.

1960s Granny. Not many like this
In such a clean and rust free state.

You must stop by to view! All chrome
As new, original fascia retained
Upholstery unstained. Passed MOT
Last week: will only swap for some-
Thing quite unique.

Very low mileage brother. As eco-
Nomical as any other. Must mention
Does need some attention. Stream-
Lined, rear spoiler. Runs on milk,
Baby oil and gripe water. Serviced -
Needs rear wash/wipe. Only one
Owner - not yet run in. Will swap
For anything.

Valerie Malory and Sue Hu Nu

Valerie Malory and Sue Hu Nu
Went to school on a kangaroo
Half way there and half way back
They met a duck with half a quack

Valerie Malory and Sue Hu Nu
Arrived at school with a kangaroo
Half way out and half way in
They met a cat with half a grin

Valerie Malory and Sue Hu Nu
Came home from school on a kangaroo
Half way here and half way there
They met a clown with half a chair

Valerie Malory and Sue Hu Nu
Went upstairs on a kangaroo
Half way up and half way down
They met a king with half a crown.

Valerie Malory and Sue Hu Nu
Went to bed with a kangaroo

Half asleep and half awake
They dreamt of
  a duck and a quack
   a grin and a cat
    a king and a clown
     a chair and a crown
     and a kangaroo
       with half a shoe!

One Worm Working

I hear one worm working
One worm working in the ground

I hear two lions lying
Two lovely lions lying down
And one worm working in the ground

I hear three monkeys making...
Three monkeys making wishes
Two lovely lions lying down
And one worm working in the ground

I hear four froggies frying
Four froggies frying fishes
Three monkeys making wishes
Two lovely lions lying down
And one worm working in the ground

I hear five bees buzzing
Five bees buzzing in the air
Four froggies frying fishes
Three monkeys making wishes
Two lovely lions lying down
And one worm working in the ground

I hear six snakes hissing
Six snakes hissing over there
Five bees buzzing in the air
Four froggies frying fishes

Three monkeys making wishes
Two lovely lions lying down
And one worm working in the
ground

I hear seven songbirds singing
Seven songbirds singing in the trees
Six snakes hissing over there
Five bees buzzing in the air
Four froggies frying fishes
Three monkeys making wishes
Two lovely lions lying down
And one worm working in the
ground

I hear eight cats kissing
Eight cats kissing on my knees
Seven songbirds singing in the trees
Six snakes hissing over there
Five bees buzzing in the air
Four froggies frying fishes
Three monkeys making wishes
Two lovely lions lying down
And one worm working in the
ground.

Brilliant

Today Mum called me brilliant
and that's just how I feel

I'll run a race
I'm bound to win
I'll take up golf
Get a hole in one

Because today Mum called me
brilliant
so that's what I must be

I'll paint a picture
A work of art
I'll design a car
It's sure to start

Because today Mum called me
brilliant
and she always speaks the truth

I'll write a song
It'll be a hit
I'll train a dog
It'll stand and sit

Because today Mum called me
brilliant
Yes, today Mum called me brilliant
Today Mum called me brilliant
So how am I feeling? BRILLIANT!

Career Opportunity: Knight Required

Are you brave, honourable
and chivalrous?
Do you like wearing metal suits
and enjoy being called Sir?
Then this could be the job for you.

Your duties will include
wielding a sword, jousting
and clanking about.

Preference will be given
to those candidates
who come equipped
with their own warhorse and squire.

If you think
you've got what it takes
turn up for an interview
and show us what you can do.

NOTE: Candidates will be left to
fight it out amongst themselves.
Castle Management accepts no
responsibility
for loss of life or limb.

I'm A Cat

I'm a cat
an ordinary cat
it's so simple
simple as that

That I'm a cat
an ordinary cat
and I do what cats do

I like to stare
and drink from a tap
I like to purr
when I'm sitting on a lap
I use my litter
when I need to poo
I do what cats do

But when I dream
I dream of mice
and I think
just how nice
it would be
if I could play
with them *Yum! Yum!*

But when he dreams
he dreams of love
he looks to the sky above
he seems confused
as if he's in a daze

But he's a man
an ordinary man
doing the best he can

It's not enough
it never is
but he's doing the best he can

But when I dream
I dream of birds
and I won't
mince my words
I would like

to get my claws
on them *Yum! Yum!*

I'm a cat
an ordinary cat
it's so simple
simple as that

That I'm a cat
an ordinary cat
and I do what cats
I do what cats
I do what cats…do!

I Like What I Like

I like the sun
I like the rain
I like the rhythm
of a travelling train
I like the shine
of a long gold chain

I like what I like
I do

I like coffee
I like tea
I like the sand
and I like the sea
I like to sink
into my old settee

I like what I like
I do

I like honey
on my bread
I like sleeping
in my bed
I like dreaming
in my head

I like what I like
I do

I like orange
I like blue
I like pizza
I like stew
I like being here
and I like you

I like what I like
I do

It's true!

I like what I like
I do!

TV Rap

After school
what suits me
is to sit on the carpet
and watch TV.

Watch TV
Watch TV
I sit on the carpet
and watch TV.

I burst in
about half past three.
Kick off my shoes
and get comfy.

Get comfy
Get comfy
I kick off my shoes
and get comfy.

Dad says, 'You're too near.
Take my advice
move further back
or you'll damage your eyes.'

But my eyes don't hurt
and they haven't turned square.
Close to the screen
is what I prefer.

When I get home
what pleases me
is to sit on the carpet
and watch TV.

I watch TV
I watch TV
and I don't budge
till it's time for tea.

Time for tea
Time for tea
and I don't budge
till it's time for tea.

When to Tease Your Sister

(after 'When To Cut Your Fingernails'
by Roger McGough)

Tease her on Monday
She'll go mad

Tease her on Tuesday
She'll be sad

Tease her on Wednesday
She'll give you a clout

Tease her on Thursday
She'll pull your teeth out

Tease her on Friday
She won't care

Tease her on Saturday
She'll wave her fists in the air

But tease her on Sunday
Without okaying it first
And your head will inflate
Like a balloon
And then BURST!

Appendix 2
Recommended Reading – a brief list

There are so many good books available, it's hard to choose. We've included Carroll and Stevenson as a reminder of classic poems. The rhyming dictionary is a brilliant tool and Dahl's Words is included to show what fun can be had continuing the Jabberwocky line. 'The Works' is there because it is crammed with examples of every poetry form you can think of. Carol Ann Duffy and Ted Hughes provide a wide range of accessible and challenging poetry. 'Friendly Matches' is full of clever and funny football poems. The Faber anthology is a seamless choice of classic and contemporary poems and Kate Wakeling is a bright new voice well worth discovering.

A First Poetry Book – edited by Pie Corbett & Gaby Morgan

Wicked Poems - edited by Roger McGough

Poetry Zone - edited by Roger Stevens

Friendly Matches – Allan Ahlberg

The Works - edited by Paul Cookson

New and Collected Poems for Children – Carol Ann Duffy

Collected Poems for Children – Ted Hughes

The New Faber Book of Children's Poems –
    edited by Matthew Sweeney

Moon Juice – Kate Wakeling

*Jabberwocky and other poem*s - Lewis Carroll

A Child's Garden of Verses – Robert Louis Stevenson

Rhyming and Spelling Dictionary – Ruth Thomson and Pie Corbett

Roald Dahl's Rotsome & Repulsant Words – Susan Rennie

Appendix 3
Useful Contacts

Arranging a Visit

contactanauthor.co.uk

authorsalouduk.co.uk

virtualauthors.co.uk

booktrust.org.uk/books-and-reading/tips-and-advice/reading-in-schools/how-to-arrange-an-author-visit

Poetry websites – for inspiration and information

Children's Poetry Archive: childrenspoetryarchive.org

Young Poets Network: ypn.poetrysociety.org.uk

The Poetry Zone: poetryzone.co.uk

Discovering Poetry: discoveringpoetry.co.uk

TweetSpeak Poetry: tweetspeakpoetry.com